Introduction

Help Me Decide! is designed as an easy-to-use resource for teachers as they work to improve behavior in middle-grade classrooms and other settings in the middle school arena. This book embraces a variety of strategies—including large- and small-group instruction, individual seatwork, group activities, and cooperative learning—and offers both novice and experienced teachers useful tools for promoting positive behavior.

The forty scenarios presented here portray realistic events experienced by many children as they attend school, travel to and from their homes, and interact with each other in their neighborhoods. Problems that surface outside the school setting are included among the scenarios because of the tendency for out-of-school troubles to affect in-school relationships and classroom performance. Positive concepts and behaviors, such as taking responsibility for one's actions, understanding rights versus privileges, and maintaining friendships, along with negative concepts and behaviors, such as disrupting class, lying, cheating, stealing, bullying, and instigating fights, are among those targeted in the scenarios.

The goal of this manual is to engage children in talking about, understanding, and beginning to change behaviors that disrupt the normal flow of classroom activities and to replace them with behaviors that enhance classroom learning. Clearly, all classroom problems cannot be solved by any one means. But research has shown that classroom discipline can be greatly improved if students are encouraged to discuss their behaviors and the behaviors of their classmates and weigh alternatives for future actions. *Help Me Decide!* provides an impetus for such discussions.

The lessons in this manual have three general objectives: to teach students how to evaluate their actions and those of their classmates and friends; to teach students that as they go about their daily routines, they usually have a range of options from which they may choose appropriate behaviors; and, finally, to guide students as they set goals for making positive changes and go on to incorporate these in their everyday lives. Most often, the steps involved in completing a lesson consist of reading a scenario, participating in group discussions, writing, role-playing, goal-setting, and self-monitoring to determine the level of goal attainment.

The cohesive factor in the wide selection of stories included in *Help Me Decide!* is the nature of the stories. They are original tales about familiar types of people interacting in familiar ways and getting into or causing trouble in the process. Lead characters (male and female in approximately equal numbers) are all young people who are grappling with problems brought on by either their behaviors of the behaviors of their friends, family members, or acquaintances. Open-ended and engaging, the stories are designed to pique student curiosity and promote discussion. Most every story in this book lends itself to a discussion of social relationships and to an analysis of the story characters' motivation to behave as they do. What begins as a general discussion of the actions of a story character soon turns into an examination of the actions of the students and their classmates.

Open-ended questions sprinkled throughout the lessons maximize discussion by asking students to analyze the lead characters' behavior, determine whether their own behavior mirrors it, and come up with suggestions for positive change. As students identify problem behaviors and attempt to aid the characters, they generate ideas for themselves or others in the class who may be in similar circumstances. While all aspects of the lessons are important, open discussion is absolutely essential to their successful completion. Desired changes in behavior have little chance of occurring if the lessons are simply used as read-and-fill-in-the-blank activities.

In addition to the stories and discussion questions, the lessons provide many other ways for students to participate—for example, by writing letters to the characters, generating alternate story endings, and even creating short role-plays. Because there are opportunities for engagement through a variety of modalities, even students who are at first disdainful of the proceedings are eventually drawn into them. Students who do not feel comfortable joining in the discussion following the reading of a scenario may, for example, take part in some later phase of the lesson, say, the role-play. This is important because students who are actively involved in the process—know their input is wanted and required, and feel their ideas are treated with respect—tend to take ownership of it. Following ample consideration of the characters and events in the scenario, the students fill out a "Goals, Strategies, and Monitoring" form for the characters and for themselves. The goals they set may be short-term or long-term and deal with behaviors in school or at home. At this time, students also select strategies for goal attainment. Students who have already met a goal suggested by a particular lesson can help their partners, group members, or the class set goals for change.

As the final ongoing activity for each lesson, students monitor their behavior to determine whether their goals have been met. In addition to successes, they note instances in which they have been unable to make changes in their behavior, and they are encouraged to consider why they failed. You, the teacher, are in a position to determine whether strategies have been followed and goals met based on (1) observations and (2) self-reports from the students. Student self-monitoring is recommended to ease the time constraints under which many teachers operate and because, in the process of self-monitoring, students will learn valuable lessons that they can take with them into new situations—particularly those in which there are no external forces urging them to do the right thing.

While completing the lessons in *Help Me Decide!* involves some extra work on the part of the teacher, the main requirement is a commitment to helping students change their lives for the better. The lessons in this manual serve as another important resource for educators in their efforts to guide young people in a positive direction. At the very least, by completing these lessons, students will have begun to examine their behavior. At best, they will have made some positive changes on which they can build as they continue in school and move beyond.

Help Me Decide!

Learning to Make Good Choices

Anne A. Boyd
and
James R. Boyd

Good Year Books
An Imprint of Pearson Learning

The scenarios included in this book are realistic fiction. All names and places mentioned herein are fictitious. None of the incidents described and discussed depicts any real or actual events taking place in classes taught by or known to the authors.

Good Year Books

are available for most basic curriculum subjects plus many enrichment areas. For more Good Year Books, contact your local bookseller or educational dealer. For a complete catalog with information about other Good Year Books, please write:

Good Year Books
299 Jefferson Road
Parsippany, NJ 07054

Book design and illustrations by Amy O'Brien Krupp.
Text copyright © 2000 Anne A. Boyd and James R. Boyd.
Illustrations copyright © 2000 Good Year Books, an imprint of Pearson Learning
All Rights Reserved.
Printed in the United States of America.

0-673-58663-4

1 2 3 4 5 6 7 8 9 - ML - 04 03 02 01 00 99

Acknowledgments

We wish to thank the many colleagues and friends who generously gave encouragement, suggestions, and reactions as this work progressed— especially Dr. Vivian Price, coordinator of the ABLE Academies, School District of Philadelphia; Robert Hargrow, ABLE Academy; Antoinette Harris and Edna Barnes, fellow teachers; Dr. Tilghman Moore, principal of Benjamin Franklin High School; and Herb Rogers, retired principal, School District of Philadelphia.

We are greatly indebted to a new friend and neighbor, Carolyn Fox, who was more than generous in lending her technical expertise to this project. Special thanks to Roslynn Mitchell for proofreading.

Contents

How to Use This Book

Each of the lessons included in *Help Me Decide!* is appropriate for groups ranging in size from a few students to a full class. For optimal results, establish a regular schedule for presenting the lessons. This way, students become accustomed to routinely examining their behaviors. At forty stories, there is more than enough material for weekly presentation.

Various academic skills are emphasized in the lessons. Students read thought-provoking scenarios, participate in open discussions, complete written activities, and engage in role-plays. They learn how to set goals for behavior change, to choose strategies for reaching those goals, and to monitor their behavior—with guidance from their teachers, of course. Students work to receive positive recognition when they make progress toward the goals they have set for themselves. If they do not work to achieve their goals, and their behavior does not improve, they suffer consequences.

Encourage your students to keep a notebook or folder of completed lessons; these can then be discussed or reviewed as necessary. Students' notebooks or folders should contain any information and forms that they will use to set goals and track their progress. While lessons and forms can be stored in class binders, this is a cumbersome alternative that places the additional burden of distribution and collection on the teacher.

The scenarios contained in *Help Me Decide!* are written at a beginning fourth- to sixth-grade reading level. Age/grade designations are intentionally omitted, however, to facilitate use of the scenarios by as wide a range of students as possible. You'll find an important word list presented in the Introductory Lesson. Review these words as needed at the outset and stress them as often as possible so that they become a part of the terminology that students understand and employ as they complete the scenarios and learn to manage their behavior. Other words that might present a problem for students appear, along with definitions, on the first page of pertinent scenarios.

The characters in *Help Me Decide!* are drawn so as to appeal to a wide range of young people. The main character in a scenario may be the student him- or herself or a fictional individual. In the former case, encourage the students to wrap themselves up in the story and become the character. When the scenario revolves around fictional characters, the students should be urged to befriend these characters, discuss their actions, note any similarities or differences between themselves and the characters, and offer the characters suggestions for change. Often, students will say that they recognize the problem being presented or

are aware of a similar problem—either way, this provides further opportunities for discussion.

Discrete question sets guide the students through the scenarios. In general, questions are formulated and categorized to direct students to first analyze the behavior of the characters and then analyze their own behavior. A question may be phrased in several different ways, or the same question may be asked about several different characters and about the students themselves. If a topic generates widespread interest and active discussion, it may be that all the questions are answered before they are asked. If this happens, simply use the questions after the discussion as a way to home in on specific aspects of the lesson.

After analysis and discussion, the students set goals for themselves, select the strategies that they will use to reach these goals, and begin to monitor their progress toward goal achievement. To supplement your own and students' ideas, see the Appendix for suggested goals, strategies, and monitoring options. The final and much-desired step, of course, is the gradual internalization of positive means and measures over time, leading to student consideration and incorporation of acceptable behavioral alternatives as a way of life.

The following suggestions for presenting each lesson represent our thinking as we prepared and tested the lessons. They are by no means exhaustive of all possibilities.

Introductory Lesson

Purpose: To teach students vocabulary related to behavior management

Question: What do we mean by self-discipline?

Procedure: Work with the whole group. Brief students on the aim of the lesson. Preview vocabulary. Have students complete the written activities. Plan additional vocabulary study. Have students begin the "Goals, Strategies, and Monitoring" form. Plan time for students to report on their success in meeting selected goals.

Students focus on the vocabulary they will use as they read and discuss the upcoming scenarios. Allow students as much time as needed to understand the words on the list. When students have completed the activities, which include a word search featuring vocabulary from the Introductory Lesson, invite them to discuss their responses.

Scenario 1 Is It Important to Arrive on Time?

Purpose: To teach students the importance of arriving on time

Question: How does lateness affect classroom learning?

Procedure: Work with the whole group. Preview the key words appearing in the lesson. Have students read and discuss each vignette and consider the importance of arriving on time. Relate ideas generated to students' own experiences. Work on strategies for improving punctuality. Help students begin filling out the "Goals, Strategies, and Monitoring" form. Plan a time to review the form and make suggestions.

Present this lesson early in the school year and revisit it periodically if lateness becomes an issue. If the students have completed the Introductory Lesson, they will already be familiar with many important behavior-related terms that may come up in the discussion. Have students list things they or their classmates can do to lessen occasions of lateness.

Scenario 2   Creating a Better Classroom Atmosphere

Purpose: To teach students to examine problems that occur in the classroom

Question: How can students help solve classroom problems?

Procedure: Begin by working with the whole group. Have students discuss the disruptive behaviors displayed in Mrs. Wiggins's class. Next, have them discuss behaviors in their own class. Then, divide students into groups and direct them to complete the written activities and discuss their ideas. Continue reviewing behavior-related vocabulary. Help students begin filling out the "Goals, Strategies, and Monitoring" form. Plan a time to review the form and make suggestions.

Students look objectively at various behaviors that disrupt a class. They first examine what is happening in the scenario and then they scrutinize their own behaviors. Finally, they think and write about ways in which they can change poor classroom behaviors. Each student chooses one negative behavior to work on changing.

Scenario 3   How Can I Get the Teacher "Off My Back"?

Purpose: To help students understand the actions of a "problem" student and the impact of these actions on the class

Question: What effect does a student such as Josea have on a class?

Procedure: Divide the class into groups. Have students list the behaviors causing Josea's "little problem" and the problems that his actions are causing in the classroom. Allow students time to compare his actions and theirs. After students have written their letters to Josea, have them share ideas within their groups. Then have them begin the "Goals, Strategies, and Monitoring" form. Plan time for students to report on their success in meeting selected goals.

Students consider various problems that contribute to poor in-school performance. Conversation among the students about Josea's actions and his attitude toward his teachers and school will lead many students to objectively scrutinize the situation; they will be able to point out, without any trouble, the things Josea should change. Students soon realize that while Josea is a likeable figure, he leaves much to be desired as a student. Discussion may turn to what Josea is doing that requires his leaving school early or not attending at all. Other aspects of his behavior away from school may come up. Ask the students if they think Josea intimidates others. Then have students examine any behaviors they exhibit that are similar to Josea's.

Through discussion, students come to understand that personal issues that they think are their "own business" can have a negative impact not only on them, but also on the class if they affect student attendance and performance. This is particularly true if the student in question has leadership tendencies, as Josea does. Further, they begin to see that a teacher who is "on their back" may be "pestering" them because he or she wants to help them make proper choices about their education in particular and their lives in general.

Scenario 4 Classroom Confusion

Purpose: To have students discuss the behaviors of a disruptive student
Question: What can one friend do to help solve another friend's problem?
Procedure: Present the lesson to the whole group. Allow students to work in pairs as they write and present their role-plays. Have them begin the "Goals, Strategies, and Monitoring" form. Plan a time when they can report on their success in meeting selected goals.

The class examines the antics of a consistently disruptive student. Most teachers have taught such a student, and most students can readily point one out. In the follow-up scenarios that students write, they are asked to seek positive outcomes. This allows caring classmates to understand that they can have a positive effect on others if they try. Through discussion and reflection, students begin to understand, as well, that disruptive behavior often conceals unresolved personal problems.

Scenario 5 Unhappy at Home

Purpose: To show students that problems from outside can affect in-school behavior
Question: How does an at-home problem become an in-school problem?
Procedure: Begin by working with the whole group. Then allow students to work in pairs as they present the role-plays and write additional ones. Have them begin the "Goals, Strategies, and Monitoring" form. Plan a time when students can report on their success in meeting selected goals.

Students discuss ways in which problems experienced outside school can become in-school problems. Some students may say that they know a person like the main character. If there is a student in the class who fits the profile of the main character, every effort should be made to protect the child's feelings during this lesson. Remember that students may identify with the main character for a variety of reasons. Typically, students respond positively to the positive action taken by the main character after his unprovoked punching of Hakeem.

Scenario 6 On Carrying a Weapon

Purpose: To help students understand the dangers of carrying a weapon
Question: What's wrong with carrying a weapon?
Procedure: Work with the whole group. Encourage students to present and explore their ideas about weapons in general and weapons in school in particular. Have students begin the "Goals, Strategies, and Monitoring" form. Plan a time when they can report on their success in meeting selected goals.

Students discuss the dangers of carrying a weapon. Recognizing that few issues in life are absolute, they grapple with the knowledge that although carrying a weapon is dangerous and can get their friend in trouble, their friend's fear of being attacked is real. In the course of helping this character work out her problem, the students come up with some worthwhile options for themselves, as well.

Scenario 7 Managing Your Anger (Two Versions)

Purpose: To help students examine positive ways of dealing with anger

Question: How can two friends change their relationship and eliminate the anger between them?

Procedure: Work with the group as a whole, or divide up the students by sex, if desired. After discussion, allow the students time to develop their role-plays. Have them begin the "Goals, Strategies, and Monitoring" form. Plan a time when the students can report on their success in meeting selected goals.

Students look at an attempt by one student to control his or her anger in the face of hurtful behavior on the part of another student. Your students may see themselves in one or more of the characters presented. They may choose sides and decide who is more like the character they perceive as the stronger one. Through discussion, they come to understand that in relationships such as those portrayed in the scenarios, both persons participate in creating the difficult circumstances in which they find themselves. Students discuss the idea that the characters must avoid fighting as a first response when they become angry. Instead, they must learn to talk about difficult circumstances and feelings and recognize that this can often bring some relief and resolution.

Scenario 8 Can I Copy Your Homework?

Purpose: To examine a negative activity that has become routine in some schools

Question: What's wrong with copying someone's homework?

Procedure: Begin by working with the whole group. Emphasize for students the point that allowing others to copy their homework is as much a part of the problem as the copying itself. Have students work in groups to complete the written work. Then have the students begin the "Goals, Strategies, and Monitoring" form. Plan a time when they can report on their success in reaching selected goals.

Students consider several important issues: copying someone else's work and claiming it as one's own, making the right choices, and handling one's feelings when a friend does not provide an immediate solution to a self-inflicted problem. Underlying this lesson is the understanding that when we make choices we must be prepared to live with the consequences.

Scenario 9   Spreading Rumors

Purpose: To help students understand the problems that rumors can cause

Question: What are some of the problems that can result when people spread rumors?

Procedure: Working with the whole group, have the students read and discuss the scenario. Encourage students to consider the problems caused when people start and spread rumors. List and discuss the options that students come up with for stopping rumors cold. Have them begin the "Goals, Strategies, and Monitoring" form. Plan a time when students can report on their success in meeting selected goals.

Students take a look at the problems caused by gossiping and not checking one's facts before speaking. Sometimes all it takes is one ill-considered statement—whether innocent or malicious—to start a rumor. The problems that result often invade the classroom, particularly if you have students who are already interested in disrupting the class. In this scenario, the problem enters the classroom very early in the day and is compounded when Jason walks in and questions Adrienne.

Scenario 10   Spitballs, Spitballs, Spitballs

Purpose: To discuss several problems created when a student throws spitballs

Question: What happens in the classroom when a seemingly minor disruption takes place?

Procedure: First work with the whole group. Have students read and discuss the scenario. Then invite them to work in pairs to act out the role-plays and write their own scenarios. Have students begin the "Goals, Strategies, and Monitoring" form. Plan a time when they can report on their success in meeting selected goals.

The students talk openly about several issues. One is throwing spitballs and the disruptive influence of this act. Another is a student's failure to take responsibility for his actions. A third is a student's refusal to acknowledge his innocence, even if it might mean getting blamed for something he didn't do. Although this lesson focuses on spitballs, the object being thrown could be an eraser, a pencil lead, a wad of paper, or any number of other things available to a student sitting in the back of a classroom.

Scenario 11   She's Going to Get You

Purpose: To teach students not to accept secondhand information as truth

Question: How should you handle secondhand information?

Procedure: Work with the whole group. Encourage students to express their ideas and feelings about secondhand information. Have them discuss the possible chain of events if the contents of a note are believed and acted upon. Have students begin the "Goals, Strategies, and Monitoring" form. Plan a time when they can report on their success in meeting selected goals.

Students discuss the actions of a note-passer and the problems that this activity can generate for others. Scenario 11 (like Scenario 12) is closely related to Scenario 9, except that the vehicle for spreading the tale is not a telephone conversation at home but a note passed during class.

Scenario 12 He's Going to Get You

Purpose: To alert students to the dangers of acting on secondhand information

Question: Why are you angry with Gilbert?

Procedure: Begin by working with the whole group. Read the scenario. Divide the students into pairs or small groups. Allow them time to complete the written activities. Discuss their responses. Have pairs or groups write role-plays or a new ending for the scenario. Then have students begin the "Goals, Strategies, and Monitoring" form. Plan a time when they can report on their success in meeting selected goals.

Students discuss the instigator, David, and his tactics. It is not clear whether the alleged perpetrator, Gilbert, has said or done anything at all. However, it is clear that if he is at home, he is going to get punched. Is it David's intention to cause a rift between you and Gilbert? Have the students discuss this possibility. Help them recognize that when someone is obviously trying to provoke you, it is often better to ask questions first than to be manipulated into taking action that you might later regret.

Scenario 13 Will You Do My Science Project? You're So Good at It!

Purpose: To help students learn how to handle a classmate who attempts to intimidate or control other students

Question: Should you expect someone else to do your work for you?

Procedure: Begin by working with the whole group. Have students read and discuss the scenario. Then divide the class into pairs or small groups for the writing of role-plays. Encourage students to view the situation from different perspectives.

Students will recognize this scenario as similar to Scenario 8. The difference here is the element of premeditation. Obviously, you, the main character, plan ahead of time to intimidate someone into doing your work. Encourage students to discuss strategies for dealing with bullies who appear to get their way year after year. Discussion may lead to a consideration of other attempts at intimidation encountered in school and to larger life issues.

Scenario 14 My Friend Makes Crank Calls

Purpose: To prepare students to deal with others who attempt to manipulate them

Question: How should a secret with serious consequences be handled?

Procedure: Work with the whole group. Have students read and discuss the scenario. Allow them time to write short notes explaining how they would handle

Sheila's request. Have students begin the "Goals, Strategies, and Monitoring" form. Plan a time when they can report on their success in meeting selected goals.

The students examine two issues: a crank caller with whom almost everyone has had some experience, and a person who, after committing negative acts, attempts to force her friend to help her avoid the consequences. Encourage the class to consider all of the options available to Deidre and to help her decide what action to take. **Note:** This lesson is related to Scenarios 15 and 16.

Scenario 15   I Received a Crank Call

Purpose: To help students discover ways to avoid reacting negatively to negative situations created by others

Question: How can a student respond positively to a negative action taken by someone else?

Procedure: Work with the whole group. Read and discuss the scenario. Have students create a list of positive options available to Jada. Then have them begin the "Goals, Strategies, and Monitoring" form. Plan a time when they can report on their success in meeting selected goals.

Students discuss the problems that can result when someone makes a crank call "just for fun." The focus is on Jada and her feelings. Students come to understand that even though Jada is justifiably upset, she should avoid taking any action that might cause her trouble in the long run; instead, she should carefully consider her options and make a sound decision about what to do.

Scenario 16   I Made Crank Calls, But I Can't Tell Anybody About It

Purpose: To help students see that they must accept responsibility for their actions

Question: What causes a person to repeatedly do something that he or she knows to be wrong?

Procedure: Begin by working with the whole group. Have students read and discuss the scenario. Then invite them to work in pairs or small groups to decide on a course of action for Sheila and Deidre. Have students begin the "Goals, Strategies, and Monitoring" form. Plan a time when they can report on their success in meeting selected goals.

Students read the confession of the person who is guilty of causing a big problem both in school and outside school. They talk about the way she tries to justify what she has done and how she attempts to shirk responsibility for her actions by asking a friend to lie for her. In so doing, students revisit the issue of a person's unwillingness to take responsibility for herself and her actions.

Scenario 17 I Know I'm Clean

Purpose: To encourage students to examine the way they treat less-fortunate classmates

Question: How can students help a less-fortunate classmate solve some of his problems?

Procedure: Begin by working with the whole group. Have students read and discuss the scenario. Then have them break into small groups for presenting the role-play and writing additional role-plays. Encourage the students to complete the "Goals, Strategies, and Monitoring" form for this lesson.

Students examine the harsh way they often treat less-fortunate students. They begin to understand that while no one wants to be around someone who is dirty or smelly, there are students who are doing the best they can without the adult input and financial support that many students take for granted. As they search for options that might be available to Jay to help him deal with his problem, they may become more compassionate and less judgmental.

Scenario 18 I Don't Want to Fight

Purpose: To help students recognize that in the case of fighting, as in almost every situation, they have options

Question: How can you keep from fighting when someone picks a fight with you?

Procedure: Work with the whole group initially. Read and discuss the scenario. Then divide the students into pairs for presenting the role-play and completing the written activities that follow. Have students begin the "Goals, Strategies, and Monitoring" form. Plan a time when they can report on their success in meeting selected goals.

Students grapple with an issue that causes problems everywhere every day: people who generate reasons to fight rather than resolve their conflicts peaceably. Through discussion, students review the idea that fighting is not the first solution to a problem. They also learn that it often takes more strength to walk away from a fight than to engage in one.

Scenario 19 Should I Take It or Leave It?

Purpose: To teach students that it is possible to avoid temptation

Question: Why is it best to be honest?

Procedure: Work with the whole group. Have students read and discuss the scenario. Relate the issues involved to their lives. Ask the students how they would react in this situation, and have them give reasons for their decisions. Have students begin the "Goals, Strategies, and Monitoring" form. Plan a time when they can report on their success in meeting selected goals.

In this lesson the students discuss three issues: honesty, organization, and time management. They review the three options presented and add others that may occur to them.

Scenario 20 Caught in the Act!

Purpose: To show students how an innocent bystander can be implicated in a theft or other crime

Question: Why is Katina surprised to see Jared in Mrs. Wiggins's classroom?

Procedure: Work with the whole group initially. Read the scenario and discuss the characters and their actions. Have the students complete the written activities and discuss them. Divide the class into pairs or small groups for writing and presentation of role-plays. Have the students begin the "Goals, Strategies, and Monitoring" form (which follows Scenario 22). Plan a time when they can report on their success in meeting selected goals.

The focus in this lesson is on the issue of stealing and the helplessness that students sometimes feel when they witness actions that make them uncomfortable. Ask students whether they believe Katina suspects Jared of stealing. Have them try to determine why Katina does not report Jared immediately. Have them consider, too, the potential for disruption if Jared is confronted in this situation.
Note: This lesson is related to Scenarios 21 and 22.

Scenario 21 It's Easy to Get Someone Else in Trouble

Purpose: To help students see that one can get in trouble without actually doing anything wrong

Question: What prevents Katina from explaining her actions?

Procedure: Work with the whole group initially. Read the scenario and discuss it. Have the students work individually to complete the written activities, including the note to Katina. Encourage them to share their work. Have students continue working through the "Goals, Strategies, and Monitoring" form (follows Scenario 22). Plan a time when they can report on their success in meeting selected goals.

During this lesson students discuss how easily one person can lie and cause a problem for another person. Talk with students about the ways in which an innocent person can seem guilty when the surprise of being accused prevents a proper and timely response. Talk too about the potential for disruption if the accused person decides to take issue with whatever is being said about him or her. Discuss any related incidents students may introduce.

Scenario 22 I Saw You Take It

Purpose: To help students understand how difficult it can be to "prove" one's innocence

Question: How will Katina convince everyone that she has done nothing wrong?

Procedure: Work with the whole group initially. Have students read and discuss the scenario, and complete the written activities. Then divide them into small groups for writing the story endings. Have students complete the "Goals, Strategies, and Monitoring" form following the scenario. Plan a time when students can report on their success in meeting selected goals.

Students deal with a young man who is a convincing liar. Have them talk about Jared and why he might be lying. Encourage the students to attempt to relate the incidents in this scenario to things that have actually happened to them. In writing their story endings, they should be sure to exonerate Katina and punish Jared.

Scenario 23 Some of My Friends Steal, But I . . .

Purpose: To encourage students to think of ways to avoid being drawn into negative behavior

Question: What can you do to help your friends understand that stealing is wrong?

Procedure: Divide students into pairs or groups; have them read the scenario and relate incidents in it to their own lives. Invite them to consider various options for solving the problem and to write a short play reflecting the outcome of one of the options. Have them begin the "Goals, Strategies, and Monitoring" form. Plan a time for them to report on their success or failure in meeting selected goals.

The goal of this lesson is to get students talking about a problem that affects many students from time to time—the efforts of their peers to convince them to do things they really may not be comfortable doing. In this scenario, the issue is stealing, but it could be any one of the many other things that young people get involved in that lead to trouble. Have students discuss strategies they can use not only to avoid temptation, but also to help their friends do the right things.

Scenario 24 I Don't Do Drugs, But . . .

Purpose: To help students develop ways to warn friends not to do drugs

Question: How can you convince your friends not to do drugs?

Procedure: Work with the whole group. Read and discuss the scenario. Have students work out a plan for approaching the problem of drug use. Suggest that they apply solutions to circumstances that they know exist among friends. Have students begin the "Goals, Strategies, and Monitoring" form. Plan a time when they can report on their success in meeting selected goals.

Students discuss drug use among themselves, their classmates, and their friends. They also consider the course of action taken by the main character, Michael Foster, as he attempts to solve a problem among his friends. Encourage students to come up with other ways Michael could have chosen to do what he set out to do. As students assist Michael, they search for ways to help friends or classmates they know who use drugs.

Scenario 25 How Much Did Your Sneakers Cost?

Purpose: To help students avoid intimidation by others who "have everything"

Question: Why are some students so concerned about how much things cost?

Procedure: Work with the whole group initially. Have students read the scenario and discuss answers to the questions. Divide the students into pairs or groups for completing the role-play and acting it out. Have students begin the "Goals, Strategies, and Monitoring" form. Plan a time when they can report on their success in meeting selected goals.

Students deal with two issues. They search for the best way to handle students who intimidate others and they devote time to the problem of students who are consumed by how much things cost. Help them see that students like Sean and Sharon succeed in intimidating more timid students largely because they have the implicit consent of most classmates in doing so. If students of good will are going to stop those who would intimidate and embarrass others, they must work together. Note: This lesson is related to Scenario 26.

Scenario 26 If I Could Just Shut Him Up!

Purpose: To teach students positive ways of dealing with others who are nuisances

Question: How can you help an annoying classmate change his behavior without getting into a fight with him?

Procedure: Work with the whole group. Have students read and discuss the scenario. Encourage them to relate the problem to their own lives. Have students begin the "Goals, Strategies, and Monitoring" form. Plan a time when they can report on their success in meeting selected goals.

Students consider the feelings of a character, Mark, who has had enough of the severe teasing and embarrassment inflicted on him by Sean. They attempt to help him find ways to accomplish his goal of stopping Sean without resorting to fighting. Students may decide that even though they are focusing on a very specific situation between Sean and Marcus, the remedies generated can be applied to other situations that they themselves face in the classroom.

Scenario 27 Is It Ever Okay to Lie?

Purpose: To have students examine the pros and cons of lying

Question: Can a lie be helpful or positive in some way?

Procedure: Work with the whole group initially. Read and discuss the scenario. Encourage students to relate personal experiences with lying. Divide the students into pairs or small groups, and have them write follow-up scenarios. Invite students to begin the "Goals, Strategies, and Monitoring" form. Plan a time when they can report on their success in meeting selected goals.

Students discuss the idea of lying as a potentially positive choice. They talk about why people lie, whether or not it is ever acceptable to lie, and whether or not they distinguish between "good" lies and "bad" lies. Following are some questions they attempt to answer: Is a lie acceptable if it is intended to help someone? Is a lie unacceptable if it hurts someone? If a lie that is told to help someone ends up turning out badly, is the lie a helpful or harmful one? Is it possible to live a normal life and not tell a lie occasionally?

Scenario 28   Has Anyone Ever "Pushed Your Buttons"?

Purpose: To help students understand that if they continually react negatively to things others say to them, they are not in charge of their own behavior

Question: Are there certain things that someone can say to you that will always cause you to react?

Procedure: Work with the whole group initially. Encourage students to discuss their "hot buttons." Allow students time to complete the written activities and discuss them. Have students begin the "Goals, Strategies, and Monitoring" form. Plan a time when they can report on their success in meeting selected goals.

The lesson here is that if we always react to things others say or do, then we are not in control—others are. Students tend to give this issue much consideration because they like to feel that no one is in charge of them but themselves. By working through this scenario, students come to learn which personal characteristics or attitudes cause them to react, with little thought, to the comments or actions of others. They discuss the class disruption that can occur if one student happens to push another student's buttons on a bad day.

Scenario 29   Taking Responsibility for Your Actions, Part 1

Purpose: To help students learn the meaning of responsibility and take responsibility for their actions

Question: Who is really responsible for what happens to Roz?

Procedure: Work with the whole group initially. Allow students to read and discuss the scenario and relate it to their own lives. Divide them into pairs for acting out the scenario and discussing their role-play. Have students begin the "Goals, Strategies, and Monitoring" form (follows Scenario 31). Plan a time when they can report on their success in meeting selected goals.

Students discuss accepting responsibility for the consequences of their actions. You may wish to have them consider this scenario in relation to Scenarios 10, 14, 16, 21, 22, and 27. Should students bring up the issue of one person's dominating, or attempting to dominate, another individual, you may wish to have them refer back to Scenarios 13, 18, and 25, where this is explored.

Scenario 30   Taking Responsibility for Your Actions, Part 2

Purpose: To teach students to accept responsibility for their actions

Question: Why would one student throw a tack at another student during class?

Procedure: Work with the whole group initially. Read and discuss the scenario, and have students complete the written activities. Divide the students into small groups and have them present the role-play. Then have them continue working through the "Goals, Strategies, and Monitoring" form (follows Scenario 31). Plan a time when they can report on their success in meeting selected goals.

Students continue to discuss the importance of accepting responsibility for one's actions. They consider the negative nature of the actions taken by the guilty student. They consider the possible harm that could have been done to the targeted student and the potential for even greater disruption of class time if the student who was hit had decided to retaliate. Finally they consider the positive nature of the targeted student's reaction.

Scenario 31 Taking Responsibility for Your Actions, Part 3

Purpose: To teach students to accept responsibility for their actions

Question: Who is responsible for the serious problem that arises?

Procedure: Work with the whole group initially. Read and discuss the scenario. Divide the students into small groups for writing the scenarios and/or story endings. Review Scenarios 29, 30, and 31. Have students complete the "Goals, Strategies, and Monitoring" form. Plan a time when they can report on their success in meeting selected goals.

Students discuss a situation—underage driving—that takes place frequently but does not generate much publicity unless tragedy strikes. Students know that the strong urge to drive sometimes tempts one to ignore requirements such as being of the proper age, having a license, and carrying insurance, not to mention obtaining permission from the vehicle's owner. Students talk about possible consequences for Alex and Jim before writing their story endings. Be sure students relate the issue of accepting responsibility for one's actions to their own lives, emphasizing in particular their in-school behaviors.

Scenario 32 Why Is Everybody Looking at Me?

Purpose: To help students deal with others whose sole intention is disruption

Question: How can one small action by one student disrupt an entire class?

Procedure: Work with the whole group. Have students read and discuss the scenario. Invite them to relate similar incidents occurring in their classes. When they have completed the written activities, have them begin the "Goals, Strategies, and Monitoring" form. Plan a time to discuss student success in meeting selected goals.

Students discuss the actions of the characters, their classmates and friends, and themselves. Encourage students to consider things they can do to avoid becoming involved in disruptive activity. You might ask them to predict what would happen if even a few students took a stand against nonsense that interrupts or prevents learning. Perhaps your students will decide to organize formally and pledge their help in attempting to solve the problems they see happening in their classes.

Scenario 33   Yo, Dude! What's Up?

Purpose: To show students the problems that can result from one thoughtless action

Question: What causes an otherwise good student to behave in a thoughtless manner?

Procedure: Work with the whole group. Have students read the scenario, discuss it, and complete the written activities. Then have the students begin the "Goals, Strategies, and Monitoring" form. Plan a time when they can report on their success in meeting selected goals.

    Students discuss the disruptive nature of one thoughtless action. They learn that the class can be held hostage while the scene plays itself out and that if they participate in the resulting confusion, they become part of the problem. **Note:** This lesson is related to Scenario 34.

Scenario 34   What Did I Do?

Purpose: To have students return to the issue of not taking responsibility for one's actions

Question: Why won't Earl admit that he is wrong for yelling into a classroom?

Procedure: Work with the whole group. Have students read the scenario, discuss it, and complete the written activities. Then have students begin the "Goals, Strategies, and Monitoring" form. Plan a time when they can report on their success in meeting selected goals.

    As in Scenarios 14 and 16, students discuss a student, Earl, who has acted thoughtlessly and is trying to have a friend, Nathan, cover for him, even though it might make trouble for Nathan. They examine Earl's reluctance to take seriously what he has done, and they talk about whether there should be a limit to what they can ask their friends to do for them.

Scenario 35   Rights versus Privileges

Purpose: To help students learn to differentiate between rights and privileges

Question: What is the difference between a right and a privilege?

Procedure: Work with the whole group. Begin by asking students to define the terms *right* and *privilege*. Then have them read and discuss the scenario. Allow your students time to complete the written activities and to discuss their responses. To extend the activity, you might ask them to expand on the list of rights/privileges and support their ideas. Have students begin the "Goals, Strategies, and Monitoring" form. Plan a time when they can report on their success in meeting selected goals.

    Students exchange ideas about the things to which they think they have a right; for many this may include expensive sneakers and other name-brand items. Encourage them to examine the effects these items sometimes have on personal relationships.

Scenario 36 Let's Get Mr. Smith in Trouble

Purpose: To impress upon students the serious repercussions of lying

Question: Why would a student lie to harm a good teacher?

Procedure: Work with the whole group initially. Have students read and discuss the scenario. Allow them time to complete the written activities. Divide the students into pairs for the role-play. Have them begin the "Goals, Strategies, and Monitoring" form. Plan a time when they can report on their success in meeting selected goals.

Students discuss the casual way in which the two characters discuss the possibility of placing the career of a good teacher in jeopardy. They talk about Jody's efforts to make trouble and Amanda's reluctance to go along with Jody's suggestions. This scenario is related to others that deal in various ways with students who lie to get their own way; see Scenarios 10, 16, 21, 22, 27, and 30.

Scenario 37 Does It Really Matter What "They" Say?

Purpose: To teach students that their ideas and opinions are as valid as anyone else's

Question: Whose opinion of you is most important—yours or someone else's?

Procedure: Work with the whole group. Have students read the scenario, discuss it, and complete the written activities. Allow them time to present the role-plays they write. Have students begin the "Goals, Strategies, and Monitoring" form. Plan a time when they can report on their success in meeting selected goals.

Through discussion, students may decide that they often allow their peers to control what they do, say, and so on. Particularly at this age, students tend to govern themselves according to what they think others might think. Students come to see that those who are the leaders often initiate actions without waiting for the approval of others. This lesson provides a good opportunity for the class to explore the issue of peer pressure and its impact on their actions and reactions.

Scenario 38 Revenge Is Mine! (Two Versions)

Purpose: To help students understand the meaning of friendship

Question: What response is best when friends fail you in some way?

Procedure: Work with the whole group. Have students read both versions of the scenario. Allow students to work in pairs to write role-plays that extend the scenario.

Students discuss friendships—what they mean and the implications of taking them lightly. They also consider possible in-school problems if the characters in question (Gerald, Ayana) decide to take action. Help students understand that some of the worst problems that occur between students in school result from animosities that develop within friendships. **Note:** This lesson is related to Scenarios 39 and 40.

Scenario 39 Ex-Friends Try to Ruin Your Party

Purpose: To teach students that they should face head-on the issues that confront them

Question: What can you do when ex-friends try to crash your party?

Procedure: Work with the whole group initially. Have students read the scenario, complete the activities, and discuss their ideas. Then divide the class into pairs or small groups for listing options and reporting back to the class.

Students discuss the concept that an unresolved issue can become a problem. They talk about why neither Gerald nor Ayana had a conversation with the friends who were talking about them in the restroom at school. Further, they talk about the things that might happen as a result of the friends' not being invited to the birthday party. Students examine their own relationships as they discuss the actions of Gerald, Ayana, and their friends.

Scenario 40 Confrontation!

Purpose: To help students develop options for dealing with potential confrontations

Question: How do you prepare yourself when you think you might be jumped?

Procedure: Work with the whole group. Have students read and discuss the scenario. Then have them complete the written activities, including the story extension.

Students discuss ways in which an unresolved issue continues to cause problems. They talk about things that could have been done to settle the issue. They suggest ways that the immediate confrontation can be handled so that everyone emerges unharmed. And they consider ways that Gerald and Ayana can renew their friendships or end them peacefully.

Introductory Lesson

As you read, consider your answer to this question:

What do we mean by self-discipline?

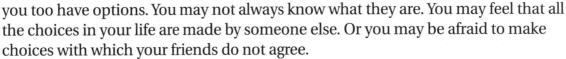 The stories that follow are about young people like you and some of the problems they face in school. You will read and talk about the way they get along with their families, classmates, and friends. In each case, try to place yourself in the situation being described and think about how you would act if you were one of the characters.

As you read the stories and discuss them with your classmates and teacher, think about all the options the characters have. Try to understand that in most of the things you do, you too have options. You may not always know what they are. You may feel that all the choices in your life are made by someone else. Or you may be afraid to make choices with which your friends do not agree.

While it's true that there are some things you cannot decide for yourself until you are an adult, there are many choices you make for yourself every day. Among these choices are choices about behavior. The lessons that follow will help you understand how to go about setting goals and choosing positive behaviors—skills that will help you now, as you go through school and throughout the rest of your life.

Focus on the Problem

Place Yourself in the Picture:

Answer Yes or No to the following questions:

1. Do things ever "just happen" to you? _____

2. Do things go wrong even when you think you're doing the right thing? _____

3. Do you find yourself in trouble without knowing how you got there? _____

4. Do you get in trouble because your friends get in trouble? _____

5. Do you get in trouble because you react strongly to things others say or do to you? _____

6. Do you get other students in trouble "just for the fun of it"? _____

7. Does your behavior sometimes lower the grades you get in school? _____

8. Is there room for improvement in your behavior? _____

If you answered Yes to any of the preceding questions, you have something to gain from the lessons that follow.

Study Some Important Words

This list contains some very special words that you will use as you complete the upcoming series of lessons. You may know many of the words already. Review the terms and their meanings.

1. **acceptable:** able to be accepted; satisfactory

   Students whose behavior in school is <u>acceptable</u> have a good chance of succeeding.

2. **attitude:** a way of behaving that shows one's thinking or feelings

   Successful students have a good <u>attitude</u> about school.

3. **behavior:** conduct; the way a person acts or behaves

   Poor <u>behavior</u> in school may lead to low grades on your report card.

4. **challenge:** to refuse to believe unless proof is given; to dare

   Have you ever <u>challenged</u> yourself to be a better student?

5. **conflict:** a fight or battle; sharp disagreement

   Sometimes having a calm discussion can prevent a heated <u>conflict</u>.

6. **confront:** to meet face to face in a bold way

   Are you willing to <u>confront</u> and solve the problems you have?

7. **consequences:** results or outcomes

   There are <u>consequences</u> for unacceptable behavior.

8. **cooperate:** to work together to get things done

   Will you <u>cooperate</u> and complete these lessons with your classmates?

9. **discipline:** training that teaches one to control behavior

   School can be more fun if students help to <u>discipline</u> themselves.

10. **disrupt:** to disturb the orderly course of events

    When students <u>disrupt</u> their classes, learning stops.

11. **esteem:** honor; high regard; respect

    Is there anyone in your life whom you hold in high <u>esteem</u>?

12. **focus:** to concentrate on one thing

    If you <u>focus</u> on improving your behavior this year, you are likely to succeed.

13. **goals:** aims; ends one tries to reach

    Set some behavior <u>goals</u> and then try very hard to reach them.

14. **monitor:** to watch in order to check up on

    If you <u>monitor</u> your behavior, you will know if you are making progress.

15. **option:** choice; the power to make a choice

    Having many <u>options</u> means having many choices in the things we do.

16. **reaction:** an action taken because of an act or a comment by another person

    You had an interesting <u>reaction</u> when your name was called.

17. **relationship:** connection

    As you grow older, try to build good <u>relationships</u> with family and friends.

18. **resolve:** to decide; to make clear

    When there is a conflict, it helps to have someone to help <u>resolve</u> it.

19. **respect:** to think highly of; to look up to

    If you have good manners, you show <u>respect</u> for those around you.

20. **responsible:** able to be trusted or depended upon

    Are you <u>responsible</u> enough to run an errand and come right back?

21. **scenario:** a very short story about the way things might happen

    You will read many <u>scenarios</u> about other students like you.

22. **self-confidence:** belief in oneself and one's abilities

    If you have <u>self-confidence</u>, you do not need to tease others.

23. **self-discipline:** act of controlling oneself and one's actions

    If you learn <u>self-discipline</u> now, it will help you later in life.

24. **self-esteem:** belief in oneself

    Gaining <u>self-esteem</u> will help you to be successful in life.

25. **self-respect:** honor or high regard for oneself

    Those who show <u>self-respect</u> usually have respect for others.

26. **strategy:** a clever plan; skill in managing any matter

    Role-playing acceptable behavior is a good <u>strategy</u> for learning it.

Complete a Word Search:

See how many of these words you can find in the following puzzle.

acceptable	confrontation	goals	respect
anger	consequences	monitor	responsible
attitude	cooperate	negative	scenario
behavior	discipline	option	self-confidence
challenge	disrupt	positive	self-discipline
choices	disruption	reaction	self-esteem
conflict	esteem	relationship	self-respect
confront	focus	resolve	strategy

```
S E L F R E S P E C T C H A L L E N G E A
A E B C D E F R E L A T I O N S H I P S C
C G L H R E S O L V E I J K F L M N O T C
O P Q F R S T U V W X O P T I O N Y Z E E
N A B C D I S R U P T I O N D E C F P E P
S A I J K I C O N F R O N T L M N U O M T
E C O R P E S A C O O P E R A T E C S P A
Q R H S E L F C O N F I D E N C E S I R B
U D U O V W X Y I Z A B C M D E F N T E L
E I H I I J K L M P N O P Q O R S E I S E
N S A U V C C O N F L I C T W N M G V P E
C R T Z G A E B C D E I F G H I O A E O O
E U T R O R E S P E C T N K B L N T N N I
S P I O A P S E L F E S T E E M I I O S R
R T T S L T T U V W X Y Z A H B T V D I A
A B U C S R E A C T I O N D A E O E D B N
E F D G H I J G K L M N O P V Q R S T L E
U V E W X Y Z A Y B C D E F I G H I J E C
D I S C I P L I N E K P O S O T I V E L S
C O N F R O N T A T I O N M R E G N A N E
```

Introductory Lesson

A. My goal is to learn _____ behavior words and meanings per _____.
   (How many?)   (day, week)

B. By _____, I will know _____ of them.
   (date)   (How many?)

C. By _____, I will know all of the words and meanings.
   (date)

D. I will use the following strategies to learn my words:

_____ complete the word-search puzzle   _____ practice using the words at home

_____ design a word-search puzzle   _____ design a crossword puzzle

_____ make up a word matching game   _____ study words independently

_____ use words orally in class   _____ use words in written sentences

E. I will monitor myself by doing the following:

_____ designing a test   _____ recording any progress in a journal

_____ taking a self- or teacher-made test   _____ counting the number of times I use the words

_____ testing my study partner/group   _____ sharing my results with my teacher

F. Comments by teacher: _____

_____

_____

_____

Signature _____ Date _____

Is It Important to Arrive on Time?

As you read, consider your answer to this question:

How does lateness affect classroom learning?

A. On the first day of *competition* at the Olympics in Atlanta in the summer of 1996, an athlete who appears to be a *contender* for a gold medal in his sport is *disqualified* for being late to his weigh-in. He explains that he went to the wrong site for the weigh-in. After discovering that he was in the wrong place, he was prevented by heavy traffic and tight *security* from getting to the proper *site* on time. This athlete had spent years training for the Olympic Games. He lost his chance to take part because he was late.

B. Every day, thousands of workers are *docked* portions of their pay because they are late for work. Oftentimes their *evaluations* are not as good as they otherwise might be because they arrive late for work. Why are these people late? Their buses are late. Their trains are so crowded that they miss their stop. Their cars won't start. Their cars have flat tires. The traffic is heavy. Their babies are sick. They are sick. Their mothers are sick. Their fathers are sick. Their pets are sick. They've lost their keys. It's raining and they can't find their umbrellas. It's snowing and they can't find their boots. . . .

C. One of your friends does a very brave thing. He goes into a burning house and rescues a baby. Everyone is very proud of what he has done. On the day that he is to receive a medal for bravery, he tries on his suit and discovers it is too small. He searches his closet for something to wear. By the time he borrows a suit from his brother, he is running late. He arrives after the presentations have been made, just as everyone is leaving. He gets his medal in the mail a few days later.

D. A patient rushes into the dentist's office and checks in at the desk. The nurse says, "Mrs. Smith, please have a seat. You'll have to wait until the doctor sees the other patients who are here."

"Why do I have to wait? I'm in a hurry! I *have* an appointment!"

"I'm sorry, Mrs. Smith, but you had a three o'clock appointment. It's now just past four o'clock. These people have appointments too. They're on time, so you will have to wait until they've been seen by the doctor. Please have a seat."

"Well, it's not *my* fault the taxi was late." Mrs. Smith looks unhappy, but she takes a seat.

E. It's a rainy Monday morning. It would be nice to stay in bed, but you really want to go to school because your classes have been very interesting lately. In one class, you're turning in your project. It's a good one and you will be proud to hand it in. But you have to hurry. You're running late. You get into the bathroom late. You don't have time for breakfast. Your raincoat is not where it's supposed to be. In your rush to get out of the house, you leave your project and have to hurry back to get it. You are at the bus stop. The bus will *not* come. When it does arrive, you can't find your token. You're going to be late. AGAIN!

---

competition: contest or match
contender: one who struggles or fights
disqualified: said to be unfit to take part
docked: to take some part of

evaluation: decision about the value of someone's work
security: something that protects
site: location

Focus on the Problem

Talk and Write About Each Story:

A. 1. How does the Olympic athlete in Story A miss his competition? _____

_____

2. What should he have done instead? _____

_____

B. What happens to the workers in Story B? _____

_____

C. 1. In Story C, what happens to the young hero? _____

_____

2. What could he have done differently? _____

_____

D. What is Mrs. Smith's problem in Story D? _____

_____

E. 1. How many reasons do *you* (the character) have for being late in Story E? _____

_____

2. Are any of them good reasons? _____ Explain your answer. _____

_____

_____

_____

Think and Write:

1. Scenarios A through E are all about the same thing. What are they all about?

   _____

   _____

   _____

   _____

2. Do you think you have a problem with lateness? _____ Explain your answer.

   _____

   _____

   _____

3. List two problems that can result in the classroom when students arrive late.

   a. _____

   b. _____

4. Make a list of things that you and your classmates can do to avoid being late to school.

   a. _____

   b. _____

5. List some things that you and your classmates can do to avoid being late when moving from class to class.

   a. _____

   b. _____

6. Complete the form that follows. Sign it and share it with your teacher.

Is It Important to Arrive on Time?

A. If my classmates or I have a problem with getting to school on time, our goal is to _____

B. These are two strategies that we (I) will use to reach that goal:

1. _____

2. _____

C. These are two things we (I) will do to monitor our (my) behavior as changes are made:

1. _____

2. _____

D. If my classmates or I have a problem getting to classes on time, our goal is to

_____

E. These are two strategies we (I) will use to reach that goal:

1. _____

2. _____

F. These are two things that can be done to monitor our (my) behavior as changes are made:

1. _____

2. _____

We (I) will practice the strategies outlined above for _____
(How long?)

If we (I) still have a problem with lateness, we (I) will change our strategies and try again.

Comments by teacher: _____

_____

_____

Signature _____ Date _____

Creating a Better Classroom Atmosphere

As you read, consider your answer to this question:

How can students help solve classroom problems?

▶ It is a *typical* day in Mrs. Wiggins's class. The late bell has rung. The class is getting settled. Mrs. Wiggins has checked the roll and the students are beginning their work. The door bursts open and Sonya enters the room. "Sorry I'm late, Mrs. Wiggins!" She talks loudly. "I had to go to the principal's office. Here's my note. What did I miss?"

Mrs. Wiggins spends a few minutes dealing with Sonya. As she finishes, Jonathan snatches a sheet of paper from his notebook, crumples it up, and heads for the trash can. He trips on Theo's feet and falls. "Sorry, man. I didn't mean to do that," says Theo.

The class goes on. Tiara has to be asked several times to raise her hand before answering questions. Tremaine strolls in without a notebook, a pencil, paper, or a note explaining why he is late.

Mrs. Wiggins stops to speak with Tremaine, who finally walks out, slamming the door. As he leaves, he mumbles something like, "Who does she think she is? So I don't have supplies or a note—so what? I'm not staying for anybody's detention."

Katrice and Mavis are told for the second time that period not to chew gum and blow bubbles in class. When Katrice is spoken to, she says, "Well, I have to go to the bathroom," as if that explains why she is chewing and blowing bubbles. "Can I go to the bathroom?"

Mrs. Wiggins is annoyed. Every time the class gets started, someone interrupts. She knows she is going to have to make some changes. What can she do to help things run more smoothly, she wonders.

She decides to ask the students to help her make a plan that will solve some of their problems. She also tells them that their first task is to try to understand exactly what they are doing that is disruptive. Their second task is to think of things they can do to change what is happening.

Mrs. Wiggins divides the class into groups. She tells the students that they will work in groups to think of a plan for changing behavior in the classroom. They will also work together on a set of class rules.

In order to accomplish these things, they must first set some goals for themselves. Then they must practice working together so that the goals they set can be reached. As the students begin to change their classroom behavior, they will be allowed to help plan the projects they will do. The students like the plan. They agree that they will work in groups to improve the ***atmosphere*** in their classroom.

---

atmosphere: the feeling or spirit of a room or other place

typical: usual, true example of its kind

Focus on the Problem

Talk and Write About Mrs. Wiggins's Class:

1. Make a list of at least four things that you think have gone wrong in Mrs. Wiggins's class.

   a. _____

   b. _____

   c. _____

   d. _____

2. Of the problems you listed in item 1, check off two problems that you feel you could help resolve if you were a student in Mrs. Wiggins's class.

Talk and Write About Options for Mrs. Wiggins and Her Class:

Think about the two problems you checked off as being ones you could help tackle. Restate each problem and offer your ideas for solving it.

Problem	Solution
a._____	_____
b._____	_____

Talk and Write About Your Actions:

Have you ever done any of the things that Mrs. Wiggins's students are doing? _____

If your answer is "Yes," identify them. _____

_____

_____

Think and Write About the Way Things Are:

1. Write a paragraph of four or five sentences describing the things you do in class that cause problems. Answer these questions as you write your paragraph:

    Do I ever do things in class that I know are unacceptable?

    Do I do these things by myself most of the time?

    Do I let my classmates talk me into doing unacceptable things?

    Have I ever talked my classmates into doing things we knew were wrong?

    What effect does my behavior have on learning in my classroom?

    _____

    _____

    _____

    _____

    _____

    _____

    _____

    _____

    _____

    _____

2. What is the single most important thing you learned about yourself in writing this paragraph?

    _____

    _____

Think and Write About the Way You Want Things to Be:

1. If you really try, do you think you can change your behavior?_____

2. What might be different if you were to make some positive changes?

    _____

    _____

Make a Decision:

Complete the form that follows.
Sign it and share it with your teacher.

Creating a Better Classroom Atmosphere

A. The behavior I will change is _____

_____

B. My goal is to _____

_____

C. The strategy I will use for reaching my goal is _____

_____

_____

D. While I work to reach my goal, I will monitor myself by _____

_____

_____

E. My target date for reaching my goal is _____

F. I have _____ to work on reaching my goal behavior.
      (How many days, weeks?)

Signature _____ Date _____

How Can I Get the Teacher "Off My Back"?

As you read, consider your answer to this question:

What effect does a student such as Josea have on a class?

▶ My name is Josea. I've got this little problem, see. Maybe you can help me solve it. It's about school and everything. It's like this. I really do like school most of the time. I mean, I get to see my friends. I think gym class is pretty cool too. By the way, I'm a pretty good basketball player. I'm on the *varsity* team. Some people tell me I could maybe play in the NBA sometime in the future.

Anyway, back to school. My grades aren't great but I'm not failing either. I don't do much homework, but I have to practice my basketball, don't I? Sometimes I carry my books to class with me, but if I know I have to leave early, I leave them in my locker. I'm training the other kids to leave theirs when I leave mine. It's easier that way.

I miss a few days of school each month and I cut out every now and then because I have things to do that can't wait until after school. You can understand that, can't you, the same as you can understand why I can't always get to class on time? Sometimes I just have to hang around a little bit and clear my head from one class to the next. Got a few buddies in class who hang with me when I let them and that's cool, too.

And sometimes when the teachers assign projects, I can't get them in on time because I don't always have the notes I need. Or I can't find some of the supplies I need—there really aren't any good stores around where I live to get school stuff. As a matter of fact, some of my classmates have started having the same problem. I think the rules should be changed to give us a break when we can't find the stuff we need.

Now when it comes down to getting along with everybody, I don't have any real problems. The little guys look up to me because they're afraid not to, and the cool guys look up to me because they know I'm cool too. And girls, well, they're no problem. As long as I call the shots, everything's okay. And nobody's complaining.

It's just the teachers. They get in my face. My homeroom teacher is *threatening* to talk to Coach about benching me because he is getting all these *negative* reports about me from the other teachers. Can you believe that? And if my grades go down any further, Coach says he'll bench me anyway because of some rule they have. What's wrong with them? How can I get them off my back? I mean, just because I get to class late and can't carry my books all the time, does that make me some kind of criminal? I can't be expected to make it to school every day, can I? Everybody misses some days from time to time. And if I don't get the notes I need or can't get the stuff I need for my projects, should I be *penalized* for it? No, I don't think so.

So, you see, I need help. What do you think? What can I do? How can I get them "off my back"?

---

negative: lacking anything positive; not good

penalized: set a penalty for; punished

threatening: saying one plans to punish or hurt someone else

varsity: the team that represents the school in games

Focus on the Problem

Talk About Josea:

1. Josea says he has a "little" problem. Do you agree with him? _____

   Explain your answer _____

   _____

2. If he doesn't find solutions to his problems, what is likely to happen? _____

   _____

3. How are Josea's actions causing problems for his class? _____

   _____

   _____

Talk About Your Actions:

1. Do you do any of the things that Josea is doing? _____

   If so, identify them. _____

   _____

2. How do your actions cause problems for your class? Give an honest answer.

   _____

   _____

Talk and Write About Your Future Actions:

1. How do you think you will go about making changes in your behavior? _____

   _____

2. Do you feel that you need help in making changes in your behavior? _____

   Explain. _____

Think and Write:

1. Think about Josea and the things he does. Tell him about one school behavior that you believe *he* should change. Then tell him what you plan to do about *your* behavior.

   Dear Josea,

   _____

   _____

   _____

   _____

   _____

   _____

   _____

   _____

   Yours truly,

   _____

2. Complete the form that follows.
   Sign it and share it with your teacher.

Text copyright © Anne A. Boyd and James R. Boyd. Illustrations copyright © Pearson Learning.

How Can I Get the Teacher "Off My Back"?

A. The behavior I want to change is _____
_____

B. My goal is to _____
_____

C. The strategy I will use for reaching my goal is _____
_____
_____

D. While I work to reach my goal, I will monitor myself by _____
_____
_____

E. My target date for reaching my goal is _____

F. I have _____ to work on reaching my goal behavior.
                (How many days, weeks?)

Signature _____ Date _____

Classroom Confusion

As you read, consider your answer to this question:

What can one friend do to help solve another friend's problem?

▶ **Read this story and complete the activities as though you yourself were confronting the situation.** One of your classmates comes into your favorite teacher's class every day and creates some kind of *confusion.* Her name is Ellen. One day she arrives late and starts an argument with the teacher when she is asked for a note. On another day, she loudly asks every few minutes to go to the bathroom.

One of Ellen's favorite ways to cause confusion is to pretend aloud that she does not understand the lesson, even though she does just fine on the days she decides to pay attention to her work. Ellen also likes to chew her gum aloud, or to talk to the person beside her, or to raise her voice to the teacher.

It almost seems that Ellen plans ahead of time what she is going to do to cause trouble each day. She is new in your school and you have only known her for a few months. But she is friendly and you like her.

No matter how you look at it, Ellen is a disruptive student. The teacher spends several minutes every day getting her settled and the class started. You know that the teacher is doing the best she can. But she has to deal with the problems of all of the students. She is a good teacher and you like her. Ellen is your friend, and you like her too, but you don't like the things she does. You want to remain her friend, but you *don't* want these problems to come up every day. What can you do? What are your options?

---

confusion: disorder

Focus on the Problem

Talk About Your Feelings:

1. Given your friendship with Ellen, how do you feel about talking to Ellen about her behavior? _____

2. How do you think talking to Ellen about her actions will affect your friendship with her? _____
   _____

3. Ellen may say that she hasn't really thought about what she is doing. If she says this, do you feel that you can help her focus on her disruptive actions? _____

   Explain how you would do it. _____

   _____

4. Ellen may say that she does not care what happens to the class. If she says this, do you feel that you can help her focus on her disruptive actions? _____

   Explain how you would do it. _____

   _____

5. How would you go about explaining to her the way that her acting up makes you feel? _____

   _____

   _____

Talk About Your Classmate:

1. Pretend that you have talked to Ellen about her behavior. What has she told you?

   _____

2. Does she seem to be willing to make changes, or does she think that her behavior is "none of your business"? _____

   _____

Think About What You Learned:

You have talked to your friend Ellen about her behavior in class. She is surprised to hear that you really don't like the things she does. She tells you that she always thought it was fun for the class if she caused problems. She says that in her old school, she did the same things and she had lots of friends there.

Ellen also tells you that she is afraid. She thinks that the other kids in the class may not like her very much because she is new. She has to do something to "fit in," she says. She has not noticed that the other students do not seem to like her disruptive behavior.

Ellen surprises you when she tells you that she is not used to taking part in class activities and doing everything the right way. She says that if she stops acting up now, the class will think something is wrong with her. She believes that if she suddenly starts to do the right thing, the others will say she is "corny" or a "nerd."

Text copyright © Anne A. Boyd and James R. Boyd. Illustrations copyright © Pearson Learning.

Talk About Your Options:

1. Now that your classmate has talked to you, what can you do? _____
   _____

2. How can you help her understand that she is okay? _____
   _____

3. What can you do to help her feel comfortable and accepted in class?_____
   _____

4. Would it be a good thing to introduce Ellen to your counselor? _____
   Why or why not?_____

5. Would it help if you talked to your teacher about the things Ellen said? _____
   Why or why not? _____

Talk About Your Actions:

1. Now that you have thought about Ellen and her problem, what will you do to
   help her fit in?_____
   _____

2. What will you do to show Ellen that being a good student is something to be
   proud of? _____
   _____

Read a Short Role-Play:

You decide to write a short role-play and ask Ellen to act it out with you. You think that if she practices acceptable behavior, it will be easier for her to get along in class. You play the part of the teacher, Mrs. Wiggins; Ellen plays herself; the class plays itself.

(Students enter the classroom. Mrs. Wiggins begins the lesson.)

Mrs. Wiggins: Good morning, class.

Ellen: Good morning, Mrs. Wiggins.

Mrs. Wiggins: Ellen, would you work as my helper today, please?

Ellen: I'd be glad to, Mrs. Wiggins. What do you want me to do?

Mrs. Wiggins: Well, first I want you to return these papers so that we can review them.

(Ellen gets up and begins to hand out the papers. She finishes and returns to her seat.)

Mrs. Wiggins: Now, most of you did well on the test, but a few of you had a problem with question number one. Who would like to give us the correct answer to this question?

Ellen: (Her hand waves in the air.) I would, Mrs. Wiggins.

Mrs. Wiggins: That's fine, Ellen. But I seem to remember that you missed number one.

Ellen: I know I did, but now I know the answer.

Mrs. Wiggins: All right, Ellen. Please stand up and answer the problem for the class.

(Ellen completes her answer and sits down. Everyone stares at her. They cannot believe what they see.)

Mrs. Wiggins: Very good, Ellen. Now, who will go to the board and explain how Ellen got her answer?

Think and Write:

1. Write another short role-play that will give Ellen another example of good classroom behavior. Have her play the part of a student who is doing the right thing. Before you begin, briefly describe what you are going to write about. _____

   _____

   _____

2. Complete the form that follows. In it, make a plan for Ellen, and make a plan for yourself should you ever do things in class to cause confusion. Share your plan with your teacher when it is complete.

Classroom Confusion

A. 1. Identify a behavior that Ellen should change. _____
_____

2. Set a goal for Ellen as she makes changes. _____
_____

3. Name a strategy that Ellen can use to reach her goal. _____
_____
_____

4. Describe how Ellen can monitor her progress as she makes changes in her
behavior._____
_____
_____

B. 1. Identify a behavior you should change. _____
_____

2. Set a goal for yourself as you make changes. _____
_____

3. Name a strategy that you can use to reach your goal. _____
_____
_____

4. Describe how you will monitor your progress as you make changes._____
_____
_____

Signature _____ Date _____

Text copyright © Anne A. Boyd and James R. Boyd. Illustrations copyright © Pearson Learning.

Unhappy at Home

As you read, consider your answer to this question:

How does an at-home problem become an in-school problem?

▶ **Read this story and complete the activities as though you yourself were confronting the situation.** You are unhappy at home. There are some problems going on there that no one has been able to solve. Often you feel sad. You have a few friends, but you don't like to have them come over because you don't know what things will be like when they get there. You don't go over to your friends' houses much because you don't know what things will be like when you get back— you might be in trouble even though you haven't done anything wrong.

If you could just find a small corner in the house that you could call your own! If only you had a place to put your things and hang out by yourself where no one could bother you, you could be happy! But things are too crowded for that. It's amazing how lonely you feel with all those people around the house. You even have to hide the poetry you write and your collection of sports cards so no one will find them.

It really isn't fair. You haven't done anything to anybody. But it sure seems like you're getting paid back for something bad. Why can't you live in a nice house like Jared's? Or have decent clothes like Hakeem's? They are both fun to be with, but it makes you a little bit angry. They've got it made and they don't even do anything to deserve it. You have better grades than they do. You are not as good at sports as they are, but they should be good because that's all they do. It just isn't fair!

You have been thinking about all of these things as you ride the bus to school. By the time you get off the bus a couple of blocks from school, you feel like punching somebody. You really would like to punch Jared or Hakeem.

As you get to the playground behind the school, you see Hakeem standing with a group of other students. He turns toward you as you get near him. He starts to say something, "Hey, man—!" Before you know it, you've punched him in the mouth so hard that he falls to the ground.

Focus on the Problem

Talk About Your Feelings:

1. Why are you unhappy? _____

_____

2. How do you feel about Jared? _____

_____

3. How do you feel about Hakeem? _____

_____

Talk About Your Actions:

1. Why haven't you talked to an adult at your house about the things that bother you? _____

2. Why haven't you talked to the school counselor about the things that are on your mind? _____

3. What has Jared *done* to you? _____

_____

4. What has Hakeem *done* to you? _____

_____

5. Why did you punch Hakeem? _____

_____

6. What consequences will you face for hitting him? _____

_____

Take a Look at Your Options:

Now that you have thought about your problems, discuss your options. Briefly describe what might happen in each of the following cases. Add and discuss other options.

1. You apologize to Hakeem. _____

_____

2. You talk to your parents or other adults. _____

_____

3. You talk to your counselor. _____

_____

Take Part in Two Role-Plays:

Role-Play 1: (Based on Option 1)

(You and Hakeem talk it over in the schoolyard.)

Hakeem: Why'd you do that, man? Are you crazy? What have I done to you?

You: I'm sorry, man. I don't know. Something just came over me. I don't know.

Hakeem: Well, you'd better figure it out because payback time is coming. I don't want to get in trouble in school, so I'm not going to do anything now. But I'll see you this afternoon down at the playground. BE THERE!

You: Okay, I'll be there. But I'm really sorry, man.

Role-Play 2 (Based on Option 3)

(You go to see your counselor as soon as you enter the building.)

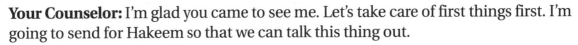

Your Counselor: Good morning, son. What can I do for you?

You: Good morning. I need some help. I punched one of my friends for no reason.

Your Counselor: I see. . . . Suppose you tell me what happened.

You: Well . . . *(You explain what happened before school. You talk a little about your home life.)*

Your Counselor: I'm glad you came to see me. Let's take care of first things first. I'm going to send for Hakeem so that we can talk this thing out.

You: I really don't want to fight Hakeem. We didn't have a disagreement going on or anything. It was my fault. I hit him. He didn't do anything to me.

Your Counselor: I understand that. We just don't want it to go any further. Later we can begin to work on the things that are *really* bothering you.

You: All right.

Think and Write:

1. Explain how you accepted responsibility for your actions in Role-Play 1.

    _____

    _____

2. Explain how you accepted responsibility for your actions in Role-Play 2.

    _____

    _____

3. Complete the form that follows. Share the form with your teacher.

Unhappy at Home

A. The behavior I will change is <u>not accepting responsibility for an action I have taken</u>.

B. My goal is to _____

_____

C. The strategy I will use for reaching my goal is _____

_____

_____

D. While I work to reach my goal, I will monitor myself by _____

_____

_____

E. My target date for reaching my goal is _____

F. I have _____ to work on reaching my goal behavior.
   (How many days, weeks?)

Signature _____ Date _____

On Carrying a Weapon

As you read, consider your answer to this question:

What's wrong with carrying a weapon?

Read this story and complete the activities as though you yourself were confronting the situation. Suppose that a classmate who is a friend of yours carries a knife in her bookbag. At school, she keeps it in her locker. At times she even carries it in her pocket. Your friend knows that she should not bring a weapon to school. And *you* know that she should not bring a weapon to school. You ask your friend why she carries it. She says she needs it because she was attacked once on the way to school and twice on the way home.

During one of the attacks, her money was stolen. The next time, she was beaten up. Your friend is really afraid to report the girls who bothered her because they say they will "get" her if she tells on them. No one seems to be able to protect her, so she feels she has to do it her-self. As her friend, you don't want to see her get into trouble. You tell her that she can be expelled from school for carrying a weapon.

You are worried about your friend. She is a good person and generally doesn't get into trouble. She says she waited for a long time before telling anyone about her problem. She trusts you so she is telling you. You want to make her feel better so you say you will try to help. Now you feel that you have to do *something*. Where do you turn? What can you do to help?

Focus on the Problem

Talk About Your Feelings:

1. Do you feel that you can really help your friend? _____ Why or why not? _____
   _____

2. Do you think you really understand how your friend feels? _____ Explain. ____
   _____

3. How do you think you would feel if someone planned to "get" you? _____
   _____

4. Is it wrong to carry a weapon? _____ Explain. _____
   _____

5. Do you feel that you should get others involved in what you want to do? _____
   Explain. _____

6. Do you think that others in your class feel the way you do but just aren't saying
   so? _____ Explain._____

Talk About Your Options:

1. What choices, or options, do you think you have? _____
   _____

2. Where can you turn for help? _____
   _____

3. Will you hurt or help your friend by taking this action? _____
   _____

4. Should you suggest that your friend report the girls who are bothering her?_____
   _____

5. Would it be better for her to tell her parents?_____ Do you think there is some
   reason why she hasn't already told them? _____
   _____

6. Can you think of any other adult who might be able to help solve your friend's
   problem? _____

7. How do you stop bullies without getting into trouble yourself? _____
   _____

8. Should you offer to help your friend fight her battles?_____ Why or why not?
   _____

Talk About Your Classmate:

1. Your friend says that no one can help her, but has she really tried asking for
   help?_____

2. Does she really think she is safe now that she carries a weapon? _____
   _____

3. Has she talked about getting hurt? _____

4. Does she worry about getting expelled from school? _____

5. How will your friend react if you tell an adult about her problem?_____
   _____

6. Does your friend's problem prevent her from doing well in school? _____

_____

Think and Write:

1. You think about what is happening to your friend. You talk to her about it. You offer to help her find some way out of her problem. You talk to your mom and dad about it. You do some more thinking about the problem, then you decide what to do. Briefly describe your plan for your friend: _____

_____

_____

_____

_____

_____

2. Complete the form that follows. Share the form with your teacher.

On Carrying a Weapon

A. The behavior my friend should change is _____
_____

B. Her goal should be to _____
_____

C. A strategy she could use for reaching her goal is _____
_____
_____

D. While she works to reach her goal, my friend could monitor herself by _____
_____
_____

E. A target date for reaching her goal is _____

F. She has _____ to work on reaching her goal behavior.
(How many days, weeks?)

Signature _____ Date _____

Managing Your Anger

As you read, consider your answer to this question:

How can two friends change their relationship and <u>eliminate</u> the anger between them?

▶ Joshua and Percy are classmates. Sometimes they are friends. When they are friends, they walk to classes together. They play ball together, usually on the same team. On weekends, the two boys can often be seen riding bikes together and just hanging out. They have known each other since first grade.

Sometimes, however, Joshua and Percy do not like each other very much. On those days, they don't want to be on the same team. Joshua says ugly things to Percy and will sometimes join other classmates to ***"bust on"*** him. They talk about his clothes, or his name, or his breath, or his mother. Joshua, on those days, says and does anything he can think of to hurt, embarrass, and annoy Percy.

When Joshua acts this way, Percy is not only hurt, embarrassed, and annoyed; he is also *very angry.* What can he do to change things? He doesn't want to get in trouble by fighting. He doesn't want to keep getting picked on. In spite of everything, he would really like to remain friends with Joshua. Why do you think Joshua acts the way he does? How can Percy make some positive changes? What options does he have?

"bust on": make fun of; say mean things about	**eliminate:** set aside as unimportant; do away with

Focus on the Problem

Talk About Joshua's Actions:

1. Does Joshua cause the problems he and Percy have? _____

   Explain your answer. _____

   _____

2. List several things that Joshua says and does that you think are wrong. _____

   _____

   _____

Text copyright © Anne A. Boyd and James R. Boyd. Illustrations copyright © Pearson Learning.

3. Are Joshua's actions those of a friend? _____ Explain your answer. _____

_____

Talk About Percy's Actions:

1. Can Percy be blamed for the problems he and Joshua have? _____

_____

2. Why does Percy want to remain Joshua's friend? _____

_____

3. What kind of person is Percy? _____

4. How do you know? _____

Talk About Your Actions:

1. Have you ever had a friend turn on you or mistreat you? _____

2. If so, how did you react? _____

_____

3. Were you able to stop yourself from getting into an argument or a fight? _____

_____

4. List some things you know how to do to calm yourself down when you get angry.

_____

_____

5. Have you ever turned on or mistreated a friend? _____

6. If so, how did the friend react? _____

_____

7. Was your friend able to stop himself from getting into an argument or a fight with you? _____

8. List some things your friend did to calm himself down when he got angry.

_____

_____

Take Part in a Role-Play:

Joshua and Percy are friends—or, at least, sometimes they're friends. Since they can still talk to each other, maybe they can begin to solve their problems. Imagine this conversation between the two boys:

Percy: Josh, I know you're in a good mood today, so let's talk.

Joshua: About what?

Percy: We need to talk about the way you sometimes act. You know—the way you talk about me, about my name, about my mom. And all that other stuff you say.

Joshua: Man, you know I'm your friend. And you know I think your mom is cool.

Percy: Well, if that's the way you feel, why don't you act like it? I mean, sometimes it seems like you're my worst enemy.

Joshua: Why do you take it that way? I don't mean any harm. I'm your friend.

Percy: You could've fooled me. Maybe you need to think a little more before you say and do things. I get so mad when you're bugging me that I feel like punching you. I would, too, but I just don't need any more trouble in school right now. I don't want any bad reports. You make me really angry, though. If you keep it up, I'm just going to punch you out and suffer the consequences.

Joshua: Well, excuse me! Why didn't you say something before? I've just been having a little fun. I didn't know I was bugging you.

Percy: Well, you were. And I don't feel like taking it anymore.

Joshua: Okay! So I won't do it anymore. Are you satisfied? I'll go bug somebody else.

Discuss the Role-Play:

1. How does Percy deal with his anger?

2. What effect does his friendship with Joshua have on what Percy says and does?

3. Could you handle a problem this way?

4. How might Percy have handled the problem if he and Joshua were not friends?

Think and Write:

1. With your group, write another short role-play for Joshua and Percy. As you write, pretend that the two are not friends. Try to have them solve the problem of anger between classmates, rather than friends.

2. Fill in the form that follows Scenario 7B. As you do so, remember that you are completing the form for Joshua and Percy. Be sure to use the information in the scenario to help you answer the questions. Share the finished form with your teacher.

Managing Your Anger

As you read, consider your answer to this question:

How can two friends change their relationship and eliminate the anger between them?

▶ Greta and Sara are classmates. Sometimes they are friends. When they are friends, they walk to and from school together. They talk on the telephone every day. On weekends, they go downtown or to the mall together. They share their secrets with each other.

Sometimes, however, Sara doesn't like Greta very much. On those days, Sara ignores Greta and joins other girls in their class to pick on her. They talk about her clothes, her hair, her house. They say someone is going to beat her up. They make up things to say about her to others in their class. On those days, Sara says and does anything she can to hurt, embarrass, and annoy Greta.

When these things happen, Greta is not only hurt, embarrassed, and annoyed; she is also *very angry.* What can she do to change things? She doesn't want to get in trouble by fighting, and she doesn't want to keep getting picked on. In spite of everything, she would like to be Sara's friend. Why does Sara act the way she does? Is she just in a bad mood sometimes, or does she have a bigger problem? How can Greta make some positive changes? What options does she have?

---

eliminate: set aside as unimportant; do away with

Focus on the Problem

Talk About Sara's Actions:

1. Does Sara cause the problems she and Greta have? _____ Explain your answer.

   _____

2. List several things that Sara says and does that you think are wrong._____

   _____

   _____

3. Are Sara's actions those of a friend? _____ Explain your answer. _____

_____

Talk About Greta's Actions:

1. Can Greta be blamed for the problems she and Sara have? _____

_____

2. Why do you think Greta wants to remain Sara's friend? _____

_____

3. What kind of person is Greta? _____

_____

Talk About Your Actions:

1. Have you ever had a friend turn on you or mistreat you? _____

2. If so, how did you react? _____

_____

3. Were you able to stop yourself from getting into an argument or a fight? _____

_____

4. List some things you know how to do to calm yourself down when you get angry.

_____

5. Have you ever turned on or mistreated a friend? _____

6. If so, how did the friend react? _____

_____

7. Was your friend able to stop herself from getting into an argument or a fight
   with you? _____

8. List some things your friend did to calm herself down when she got angry.

_____

Take Part in a Role-Play:

Sara and Greta are friends—or at least, sometimes they're friends. Since they can still
talk to each other, maybe they can begin to solve their problem.

Greta: Sara, we need to talk about the way you act sometimes. You know—the way
you talk about me, my hair, and my house, the way you say someone is going to beat
me up.

Text copyright © Anne A. Boyd and James R. Boyd. Illustrations copyright © Pearson Learning.

Sara: Oh, Greta, you know I'm your friend. You know I don't mean any harm.

Greta: Well, if you feel that way, why don't you act like it? I mean, sometimes you act like my worst enemy.

Sara: Why do you take it that way? I'm just kidding you when I do that.

Greta: Well, you could've fooled me. Maybe you need to stop and think about how it would feel if I did the same thing to you.

Sara: You wouldn't do that.

Greta: You don't know what I'll do. I know one thing. If you keep on saying stuff about me and making me angry, I might wind up punching you in the mouth. I'll just beat you up and suffer the consequences.

Sara: Well, excuse me! Why didn't you say something before? I've just been having a little fun. I didn't know I was bugging you.

Greta: Well, you have been. You've been making me angry. I don't like feeling that way.

Sara: Oh, it was just something to do. And the other kids were doing it and you didn't seem angry.

Greta: I know they were. But they're not my friends. You're supposed to be my friend.

Sara: I'm really sorry, Greta. I didn't mean to hurt you. I really don't know why I act like I do sometimes. Maybe if you had said something before . . . well, anyway, I'm sorry.

Discuss the Role-Play:

1. How does Greta deal with her anger?

2. What effect does her friendship with Sara have on what says and Greta does?

3. Could you handle a problem this way?

4. How might Greta have handled the problem if she and Greta were not friends?

Think and Write:

1. With your group, write another short role-play for Sara and Greta. This time, pretend that the two are not friends—that is, have them solve the problem of anger between classmates. Before you begin, briefly describe what you are going to write about.

2. Fill in the form that follows. As you do so, remember that you are completing the form for Sara and Greta. Be sure to use the information in the scenario to help you answer the questions. Share the finished form with your teacher.

Managing Your Anger

A. 1. Identify a behavior that Joshua/Sara should change. _____

_____

2. Set a goal for Joshua/Sara to aim for as he/she makes changes. _____

_____

_____

3. Name a strategy that Joshua/Sara can use to reach his/her goal. _____

_____

_____

4. Tell Joshua/Sara how to monitor his/her progress as he/she makes changes in his/her behavior. _____

_____

_____

B. 1. Identify a behavior that Percy/Greta should change._____

_____

2. Set a goal for Percy/Greta to aim for as he/she makes changes. _____

_____

_____

3. Name a strategy that Percy/Greta can use to reach his/her goal. _____

_____

_____

4. Tell Percy/Greta how to monitor his/her progress as he/she makes changes in his/her behavior. _____

_____

_____

Signature _____ Date _____

Can I Copy Your Homework?

As you read, consider your answer to this question:

What's wrong with copying someone's homework?

(Scene 1: Friday after school)

"How do you like that? It's Friday and we get homework," complains Jason as he walks home from school with Charlie.

"I know, man. On the weekend," replies Charlie. He thinks for awhile. Then he says, "We do need to work on this math, though. We've got a big test coming up."

Jason replies, "Yeah."

They walk on, quietly going over all the work they have to do. They think about how it will ruin the weekend. There is going to be a lot going on at the *recreation* center this weekend and it's a shame to have to miss it all. They reach the corner, where they go their separate ways. Charlie says, "Well, I suppose we'll be too busy doing our math to fit in very much basketball this weekend. But maybe we can study together. I'll give you a call."

"Yeah, man," mumbles Jason. "See you later." He is getting angrier and angrier as he walks along. By the time he gets home, he has made up his mind. He is going to do the things he has planned to do all along. Later for math.

(Scene 2: Jason's house)

When Jason arrives home, his mother says, "There's a snack for you in the kitchen. Why don't you have it before you begin your homework?"

"Thanks for the snack, Mom," says Jason, "but I don't have any homework."

(Scene 3: Monday morning at school)

"Hey, man," says Charlie. "I tried to call you all weekend so we could get together on that math. But you weren't ever at home when I called. What happened to you, Jason?"

"Oh, I was busy. But I had fun. I made the first team over at the center. If you had been there, you probably would've made it too. I was going to call you this morning, but I got up late so I didn't have time. I need to copy your math homework. I can start copying it during home-room period and finish it at lunchtime."

Charlie stops walking and frowns. "No, man, no. I spent the whole weekend solving those math problems. I can't give them to you just like that."

"But I really need to copy them. I don't want to go in there without homework," says Jason.

"You should have thought about that over the weekend," Charlie replies. "I wanted to play basketball, too, but I did my work instead. I'm not giving you my math."

"But we're friends," Jason says. "It's just some math. What's the big deal?"

> **recreation:** play, fun, games

Focus on the Problem

Talk About Charlie's Actions:

1. What kind of person does Charlie seem to be? _____

   _____

2. Why does Charlie feel angry about letting Jason copy his homework? _____

   _____

Talk About Jason's Actions:

1. What kind of person does Jason seem to be? _____

   _____

2. Why does Jason feel that Charlie should allow him to copy his homework? _____

   _____

Talk About How You Feel:

1. What is the "big deal" about sharing homework? _____

   _____

2. How do you feel about letting others copy your homework?_____

   _____

3. If, in the future, someone asks you for your homework, what will you do?

   _____

4. How do you feel about copying someone else's homework? _____

   _____

Talk About Options for Your Class:

1. In your opinion, is sharing homework a problem in your class?_____
   _____

2. If it is, can you help figure out a way to solve this problem? _____
   _____

Think and Write About Your Options:

1. Briefly describe what might happen in each of the following cases. Add and discuss other options.

   a. The class takes a pledge not to share or copy homework._____

      _____

   b. The students sign a contract with the teacher agreeing not to copy or share homework._____

   c. (Other option) _____

   d. (Other option) _____

2. Fill in the form that follows. Share it with your teacher when it is complete.

Can I Copy Your Homework?

A. My goal is to _____

_____

    1. If I have been letting others copy my homework, I will _____

       _____

       _____

    2. If I have been copying other people's homework, I will _____

       _____

       _____

B. These are two strategies that I will use to reach that goal:

    1. _____

       _____

    2. _____

       _____

C. I will monitor my progress by _____

_____

_____

_____

D. My target date for reaching my goal is _____

E. I have _____ to work on reaching my goal behavior.
    (How many days, weeks?)

Signature _____ Date _____

Spreading Rumors

As you read, consider your answer to this question:

What are some of the problems that result when people spread rumors?

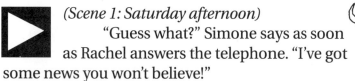 *(Scene 1: Saturday afternoon)*
"Guess what?" Simone says as soon as Rachel answers the telephone. "I've got some news you won't believe!"

"What is it?" Rachel asks.

"Do you know Adrienne, who lives over near the park? From Mrs. Parker's class?"

Rachel replies, "Yes, I know her, but I didn't know you knew her."

"I don't, but I just got some news about her. Do you want to hear it or not?"

"Okay."

"She's going to have a baby!"

"A baby?" Rachel doesn't quite know what to say about the information she has just received. "How do you know that?"

"Doesn't matter how I know. I just know. What's wrong with you?"

"Nothing. I just can't imagine Adrienne with a baby, that's all."

"Well," Simone says **sarcastically,** "they have them every day."

"Oh, I know that. But she's so smart. They say she's just about the smartest girl in our school, and even though college is a long way off, her church has already promised her a scholarship. I'm just surprised, that's all."

"Well, don't be. It happens to the best of us. Talk to you later."

(Scene 2: Sunday afternoon)
"Guess what?" Simone says as soon as Tricia answers the telephone. "I've got some news for you. You're going to be shocked! Do you remember Adrienne, who was in our class last year?"

Tricia answers, "Yes."

"Well, let me tell you what I found out. . . ."

(Scene 3: Monday morning at school)
(The door to Mrs. Parker's homeroom opens and Adrienne walks in. Everybody stares at her. She sits near her friend, Stacey, feeling a little strange.)

"Why is everyone staring at me?" Adrienne whispers to Stacey. "Do I look all right?"

"You look fine, but we've all heard the **rumor** about your baby. Why haven't you told me you're having a baby?"

"Having a baby? Me? I'm not having a baby! What ever gave you that idea?"

"That's what Vivian told me. She said Simone told her."

"I can't believe they're saying that. I'm not having any babies for a long time. I'm going to college."

"But what made them think you were having a baby?"

"I don't know. Maybe it's because I went to the doctor on Saturday with my mom. She's having a baby. My dad is real happy because it's going to be a little boy. I'm happy because I'll finally have a little brother. But just wait until I catch up with Simone!"

(The door opens and Jason walks into homeroom. He looks across the room, sees Adrienne, and starts talking aloud.)

"Yo, Adrienne! They tell me you're having a baby. Is it true?"

rumor: gossip; untrue stories that are told as true stories	**sarcastically:** in a mocking or sneering way to make someone feel foolish

Focus on the Problem

Talk About Simone's Actions:

1. What has Simone managed to do over the course of one weekend? _____

   _____

2. What do Simone's actions tell you about her? _____

   _____

   _____

Talk About Rachel and Tricia:

1. Do Rachel and Tricia seem to be really interested in the "news" Simone gives them? _____ Explain. _____

2. What could they have said that would have stopped Simone from spreading her "news"? _____

Talk About Adrienne:

1. What do you think Adrienne is going to say to Simone? _____

   _____

2. Will Adrienne be able to explain to her classmates what really happened?

   _____

3. What will she say to them? _____
_____

Talk About Your Feelings:

1. How do you feel about what Simone has done? _____
_____

2. Has someone ever started a rumor about you? _____ If so, explain what happened. _____
_____
_____

3. How did you feel when you learned about the rumor? _____
_____

Talk and Write About Your Actions and the Actions of Your Classmates:

1. What can happen in the classroom when someone starts a rumor? _____
_____

2. How can you and your classmates stop rumors from getting started in your classroom? _____
_____

Talk and Write About Options for You and Your Classmates:

1. Working with your classmates, come up with two options you have for stopping rumors. Briefly describe what you think would happen if each one were carried through.

   Option a: _____
   _____

   Option b: _____
   _____

2. Complete the form that follows. Share it with your teacher when you are finished.

Spreading Rumors

A. My goal for stopping the spread of rumors is to _____

_____

B. The strategy I will use for reaching my goal is _____

_____

_____

C. I will monitor my progress toward my goal by _____

_____

_____

D. My target date for reaching my goal is _____

E. I have _____ to work on reaching my goal behavior.
(How many days, weeks?)

Signature _____ Date _____

Spitballs, Spitballs, Spitballs

As you read, consider your answer to this question:

What happens in the classroom when a seemingly minor disruption takes place?

It's a clear, bright day. Reginald goes to school in a happy mood. He has been doing well so far. His grades have been good. His parents have told him that if he continues to do well and his report card is good, he can plan on getting that computer game he wants and maybe a few other things besides. They have said that his grades in behavior count as much as his grades in his subjects.

Everyone in school knows that Reginald has had problems in the past. But this year is different. He has decided to make some positive changes and has been working very hard to remain true to his word.

Reginald's wonderful day soon changes for the worse. During first period, a classmate who is sitting next to him makes and throws a few spitballs. Nothing happens. In a few minutes, his classmate makes and throws some more spitballs while the teacher is *distracted.*

A student near the front of the room is hit by a spitball. He turns and yells at Reginald, accusing him of throwing spitballs. "You'd better stop. If you hit me again, I'm going to get up and clobber you. I'm not taking that from you!" To the teacher he says, pointing at Reginald, "He hit me with a spitball!"

Reginald sits staring at the teacher, feeling helpless. He can't believe what is happening. Nathaniel, who threw the spitballs, is busily working. Why doesn't he speak up and say he did it? The teacher looks at Reginald as if trying to decide whether he is guilty or not. Reginald wants to say he didn't do it, but the words won't come out. He knows his teacher is a *no-nonsense* person who believes that you either earn an A in behavior or an F, because you're either doing the right thing or you're not.

Finally, the teacher says quietly, "Reginald, I'd like to see you for a few minutes when the class ends."

distracted: when distracted, one's attention is drawn to something else	**no-nonsense:** serious; accepting no silliness

Focus on the Problem

Talk About Reginald's Feelings:

1. How do you think Reginald feels about being accused of something he did not do?

   _____

2. How do you think he feels about the student who accused him unfairly? _____

   _____

3. How do you think Reginald will feel if he is punished for something he did not do?

   _____

4. Do you think Reginald feels it is wrong to tell on someone who is causing trouble? _____ Why do you think that?_____

   _____

Talk About Nathaniel's Actions:

1. Why doesn't Nathaniel speak up and say he threw the spitballs? _____

   _____

2. What effect, if any, do students like Nathaniel have on your classroom? _____

   _____

Talk About Reginald's Actions:

1. What do you think Reginald is planning to say to the teacher after class? _____

   _____

2. What do you think Reginald will do if he tells on Nathaniel and Nathaniel challenges him? _____

   _____

3. What do you think Reginald will do if the teacher doesn't believe him? _____

   _____

Talk About Reginald's Options:

1. Do you think Reginald will be able to convince the teacher that he has done nothing wrong? _____ Explain. _____

   _____

2. Will he be willing to stand up to Nathaniel and other students in the class who cause trouble? _____ Explain. _____

   _____

3. Will he get other students to stand with him? _____ Explain. _____

_____

Talk About Reginald's Classmates:

1. Do Reginald's classmates seem to have a problem with spitballs, or do they think spitballs are okay? _____

_____

2. What can Reginald and his classmates do to convince spitball throwers that what they are doing is disruptive?_____

_____

3. What power do Reginald and his classmates have to help solve problems like this in the classroom? _____

_____

Take Part in Two Role-Plays:

Role-Play 1 (Based on Option 1)

(After class, Reginald walks to the teacher's desk.)

Reginald: You wanted to talk to me?

Teacher: Yes. I'm concerned about the spitball throwing. Do you know who is throwing them?

Reginald: Yes, sir. I know who is throwing them. But I don't want to tell on him.

Teacher: Why?

Reginald: Well, for one thing, if I do, he'll know I told on him. And then I'll have some problems with him. I'm trying to do the right thing this year. I can take care of myself, but I don't want any trouble.

Teacher: I understand that and I respect it. I've noticed that you have been working very hard this year. I did not ask you to stay behind in order to have you tell me who is throwing spitballs. I just want to assign you to a different seat.

Reginald: Why are you moving me? I haven't done anything.

Teacher: I agree. I'm moving you so you can't be blamed when Nathaniel throws more spitballs. I have to catch him at it. It has to be clear who is doing the throwing.

Reginald: All right. No problem.

Role-Play 2 (Based on Option 2)

(After school, Reginald meets Nathaniel.)

Reginald: Nathaniel, I've got a few things to say to you.

Nathaniel: What, man?

Reginald: You know, you have to stop that spitball junk. I almost got in trouble today because of you. I didn't tell on you because I'm not in it. And I just want to make sure it stays that way.

Nathaniel: What's your problem, man? All I'm doing is having a little bit of fun. You can't tell me what to do.

Reginald: I can if what you do might get me in trouble. I don't care what you do on your own time, but leave me out of it.

Nathaniel: So when did you get to be an angel? We used to throw spitballs together last year. You threw more than I did.

Reginald: You're right. But that was last year. I grew up a little. I know that throwing spitballs is a dumb thing to do. It took me a while to figure it out, but I have. And I don't want anybody getting me in trouble.

Nathaniel: Well, I still say you can't tell me what to do.

Reginald: All I'm saying, man, is back off. Don't get me caught up in your nonsense.

Think and Write:

1. Explain what took place in the first role-play. _____

   _____

   _____

   _____

2. Explain what took place in the second role-play. _____

   _____

   _____

   _____

3. Complete the following form, in which you choose goals and strategies for both Nathaniel and yourself. Share it with your teacher when you are done.

Spitballs, Spitballs, Spitballs

A. 1. Identify a behavior that Nathaniel should change. _____

_____

2. Set a goal for Nathaniel to aim for as he makes changes. _____

_____

_____

3. Name a strategy that Nathaniel can use to reach his goal. _____

_____

_____

4. Tell Nathaniel how to monitor his progress as he makes changes in his behavior. _____

_____

B. 1. The behavior I am going to change is _____

_____

2. The goal I am going to work toward as I make changes _____

_____

_____

3. The strategy I will use to reach my goal is _____

_____

_____

4. I will monitor my progress as I make changes in my behavior by _____

_____

_____

Signature _____ Date _____

She's Going to Get You

As you read, consider your answer to this question:

How should you handle secondhand information?

▶ **Read the story and complete the activities as though you yourself were confronting the situation.** You are in English class when Tracy passes you a note. You are busy doing your assignment and copying your homework, so you don't read the note until you get to the lunchroom. You can't believe what it says:

Shanice says she's going to get you because
you think you are cuter and better than anybody else.
She says she used to be your friend
but she doesn't like you anymore because she has
seen you talking to Ross and she likes him. And
besides, she says you talk about her behind her
back. P.S. Don't tell her I told you.
                    Signed,
                    Me

You look around the lunchroom for Tracy. You don't see her but you do see Shanice sitting at another table. When she sees you, she smiles and waves. You just stare at her. You don't know whether to smile or wave back. What could have happened? You were supposed to be her good friend. *She* was always the one who said *you* were cute. Besides, Ross is a friend of yours. You knew him before you knew Shanice. You just don't get it. What should you do?

You look up from your lunch and Shanice is walking toward your table. . . .

Focus on the Problem

Talk About Tracy:

1. What is Tracy up to? Why would she write such a note? _____

   _____

2. Is she honest? _____ Can she be depended on? _____

   _____

Talk About Shanice:

1. Is she the kind of person who would say the things Tracy talks about in the note? _____ Explain. _____

2. Would it be good to have a quiet talk with Shanice? _____
Explain. _____

3. If you talk to her, what do you expect her to say? _____

Talk About Your Feelings:

1. How do you feel about talking with Shanice about the note? _____

_____

2. Should you ask Tracy what's going on? _____

_____

3. Should you just forget about the whole thing? _____

_____

Think and Write About Your Options:

1. After reviewing what has happened, what options do you feel you have?

   a. _____

   b. _____

   c. _____

2. Compare your list of options with the list that follows.

   Option a. Forget what happened.

   Option b. Talk to Tracy.

   Option c. Talk to Shanice.

   Option d. Talk to Ross.

   Option e. Talk to a counselor.

3. Describe what you think would happen if each of these options was carried through.

   a. _____

   _____

   b. _____

   _____

c. _____

_____

d. _____

_____

e. _____

4. Read the following note and decide whether you should send it to Tracy or forget it. Use the space provided to explain your reasoning.

> Dear Tracy,
>   I am writing to you because you wrote to me. I don't believe what you wrote is true, so I am just going to forget all about it. If you have anything to tell me, I think you should just say it to me. I don't like to pass notes in class, and I don't like to talk about my friends. Please don't write me any more notes.
>
>   _____

_____

_____

_____

_____

5. Are you a note passer? If so, plan to make some changes. Complete the form that follows Scenario 12.

He's Going to Get You

As you read, consider your answer to this question:

Why are you angry with Gilbert?

 Read the story and complete the activities as though you yourself were confronting the situation.
You and your buddy David are walking home from school one day when he begins telling you some things he says your buddy Gilbert said about you. "He did too say he was going to get you!" yelled David. "We were walking home from the playground and I heard him tell that other guy—I don't know his name, but they call him 'Muff'— anyway, I heard him say he's going to get you if it's the last thing he ever does."

"He said you tried to show him up on the basketball court. Then he said you're just a hot dog and he can outplay you any day. He said he's going to wait until you're in class one day so everybody can see him put you in your place. And then he said he might just jump you in the lunchroom so he can *really* show you up. Then your girl will see you aren't worth much."

You walk along getting angrier and angrier all the time. At first you try to defend your buddy Gilbert—at least, he used to be your buddy. You two have been tight for a long time. You can't imagine having a fight with him. But then, after thinking about all the things he said about you, you're just about ready to punch him out. As a matter of fact, you won't wait until he challenges you in school. You know where he lives, so you are going—you'll just go over to his house *now*. You're going to call him out and settle this matter once and for all.

By now, you're walking faster than David. He's hurrying to keep up.

"See you, man. I've got to split," you say over your shoulder to David. You walk up to Gilbert's house and ring the doorbell, hoping he answers the door.

Focus on the Problem

Talk About David:

What is David doing?_____

_____

Talk About Gilbert:

1. What is the relationship between Gilbert and David?_____

_____

2. What is the relationship between you and Gilbert?_____

_____

Make a Judgment:

1. If you get into a fight with Gilbert, who will be the winner—you, Gilbert, or David? _____ Explain. _____

_____

2. Is there a chance this problem will carry over into school the next day? _____

Explain. _____

_____

Talk About Consequences:

1. What is likely to happen if you go to Gilbert's house and punch him?_____

_____

2. What is likely to happen if you beat David up for gossiping?_____

_____

3. When someone says or does something that annoys you, do you think about possible consequences before taking action? _____ Explain. _____

_____

Think and Write:

1. With a partner or your group, write three different role-plays.

   a. In the first one, you go to Gilbert's house and have a discussion with him.

   b. In the second one, you go to David's house and have a discussion with him.

   c. In the third one, you talk with David and Gilbert at the same time and decide whether or not the conversation between David and Gilbert really took place.

2. With a partner or your group, write three new endings for the original scenario. Use the role-plays you wrote as guides.

3. Decide which of the three endings is most positive and causes the fewest problems.

4. Complete the form that follows. Sign it and share it with your teacher.

She's Going to Get You (Scenario 11)

He's Going to Get You (Scenario 12)

A. The behavior I will change is _____
_____

B. My goal is to _____
_____

C. The strategy I will use to reach my goal is _____
_____
_____

D. While I work to reach my goal, I will monitor myself by _____
_____
_____

E. My target date for reaching my goal is _____

F. I have _____ to work on reaching my goal behavior.
(How many days, weeks?)

Signature _____ Date _____

Will You Do My Science Project? You're So Good at It!

As you read, consider your answer to this question:

Should you expect someone else to do your work for you?

▶ **Read the story and complete the activities as though you yourself were confronting the situation.** It happens every year. You don't mind doing regular schoolwork. In fact, you think school is pretty okay. But then after a few weeks, all the projects pile on. You know they're coming, so you might as well get ready. Let's see, you have to do a social studies project, an English project, a shop project, and a science project.

You'll do the social studies, English, and shop projects. But wait a minute! You draw the line at science. You don't do science projects. It's not that you can't do them. You can do anything you put your mind to. But you just don't do science projects. You really don't like science, period. Science projects take too much time and you have too many other things to do. And this year, you don't even like the science teacher. Later for science projects.

So now, who's going to be lucky enough to do your project for you this time? It's going to be a little harder to find somebody this year than it was last year. You have to pick just the right person. Whoever does it for you has to be smart enough to do two projects, and just scared enough to keep it a secret. Let's see, now. . . .

Focus on the Problem

Talk About Your Actions:

1. Why are you getting someone to do your work for you?_____

_____

2. Is this the kind of thing you have done before? _____ Explain. _____

_____

3. Have you had any trouble in the past trying to find someone to do your projects?

Explain. _____

_____

4. Why should someone be willing to do your work for you?_____
   _____

5. Do you think that what you are doing is wrong? _____ Explain. _____
   _____
   _____

6. Would you do someone else's work if you were asked? _____ Why or why not?
   _____

7. What is the real reason that you don't do your own science projects? _____
   _____

8. What will you do if you can't find anyone to do your project for you? _____
   _____

Talk About a Person Who Expects Others to Do Work for Him/Her:

1. What kind of person wants others to do work for him/her? _____
   _____

2. What kind of attitude does this person seem to have? _____
   _____

3. How can somebody stand up to a person like this? _____
   _____
   _____

Talk About the Person Who Does Another's Work for Him/Her:

1. Describe the kind of person who agrees to do someone else's work for him/her.
   _____

2. Might such a person be afraid *not* to do the work? _____ Explain. _____
   _____

Think and Write:

Pretend that a classmate has asked you to do his project for him. With your partner or group, write a short role-play in which you tell the person that you will not do anyone's work but your own.

My Friend Makes Crank Calls

As you read, consider your answer to this question:

How should a secret with serious consequences be handled?

▶ Dear Diary,

I am writing this note to you because I can't tell a real person what's on my mind right now. First, I have to figure out what to do. Maybe you can help me think it through. Here's what has been happening. In the last few weeks, someone has been making crank phone calls to the homes of students in our school. Over the weekend, five or six people I know got these calls.

Some of the calls have been silly. Probably the people who get them don't think so, though. Anyway, everybody has been laughing about them. Like the call to this boy whose last name is "Hamm." It went something like this:

"Hello. Is this Hamm? Oh, it is? Well, my name is Eggs and I'd like to have you on my plate any day. Ha ha."

A call to Jada's house caused a real problem, though, because the caller said she worked at a funeral home. Before she could say anything else, Jada's grandmother fainted. You see, Jada's grandfather had been taken to the hospital that afternoon and her grandmother thought something might have happened to him. The caller hung up quickly.

Imagine my surprise when I discovered that it's my friend Sheila who has been making the calls! She told me about it because she's afraid she's going to get caught. She wants me to help her cover up what she did by saying she spent last weekend with me. She wants me to say we were together the whole time and she couldn't have made any calls without my knowing about it. Sheila is my friend and I don't want to see her get in trouble. But I think it was wrong for her to do what she did. And I sure don't want to get in any trouble for helping her. What can I do? What *should* I do?

Sincerely,
Deidre

Focus on the Problem

Talk About What Is Happening:

1. What is happening in this scenario?_____
   _____
   _____

2. Is Sheila breaking the law by making these calls? _____
   _____

Talk About Sheila:

1. Why has Sheila admitted to making the calls? _____
   _____

2. Does she seem to be willing to take responsibility for what she has done? _____
   _____

Talk About Your Feelings:

1. How do you feel about what Sheila is doing? _____
   _____

2. If a friend asks you to lie, do you feel that you have to do it? _____
   Explain. _____

Talk About Deidre's Options:

1. Should Deidre tell her parents what Sheila has done? _____ Explain. _____
   _____

2. If she does, what do you think they might say or do? _____
   _____

3. Should Deidre talk to her counselor at school? _____ Explain. _____
   _____

4. If she does, what kind of action do you think the counselor might take? _____
   _____

Think and Write:

1. Write a short note to Deidre telling her what you think she should tell Sheila.
   Dear Deidre,

   _____

   _____

   _____

   _____

   Yours truly,

   _____

2. Complete the following form. Share it with your teacher.

My Friend Makes Crank Calls

A. Identify a behavior that Sheila should change. _____
_____
_____

B. Set a goal for Sheila to work toward as she makes changes._____
_____
_____

C. Name a strategy that Sheila can use to reach her goal. _____
_____
_____

D. Tell Sheila how she can monitor her progress as she makes changes. _____
_____
_____

Signature _____ Date _____

I Received a Crank Call

As you read, consider your answer to this question:

How can a student respond positively to a negative action taken by someone else?

 My name is Jada. I'm a good person. Well, I admit I've had my share of problems, but they're mostly behind me now. Right at this moment, though, I'm really angry. I'll tell you why.

At school, they've been talking about the crank calls that everybody has been getting. I haven't said much. I've been minding my own business and listening to what everyone else has been saying. I want to try to find out who has been making the calls. I think that if I just listen hard enough, I'll figure it out. I'm getting to why I'm so angry. . . .

You see, somebody called my grandmother and made a sick joke about my grandfather, who is in the hospital. Grams was so upset she fainted. I wish I had answered that telephone. I would've made that person sorry she called. I'm still trying to find out who did it. When I do, I'm going to deal with her. I can't wait to get my hands on her. Nobody messes with my Grams!

Focus on the Problem

Talk About Jada's Options:

1. If Jada finds out who made the call, should she let an adult at school handle the matter? _____ Explain. _____

   _____

2. Should she try to solve the problem herself? _____ Explain. _____

   _____

Talk About Jada's Actions:

1. Now that Jada has had a chance to think about her options, what do you think she will do when she finds out who made the call? _____

   _____

2. Complete the following form for Jada. Share it with your teacher.

I Received a Crank Call

A. Identify a behavior that Jada should change. _____

_____

_____

B. Set a goal for Jada to work toward as she makes changes. _____

_____

_____

C. Name a strategy that Jada can use to reach her goal. _____

_____

_____

D. Tell Jada how she can monitor her progress as she makes changes. _____

_____

_____

Signature _____ Date _____

I Made Crank Calls, But I Can't Tell Anybody About It

As you read, consider your answer to this question:

What causes a person to repeatedly do something that he or she knows to be wrong?

My name is Sheila. I'm the one who has been making those crank calls everybody is talking about. I don't know how I got started making the calls this time. The only other time I ever did it was one night a long time ago when I had a sleep-over party. My friends and I played a few telephone tricks on people. We thought it was fun and we laughed about the way people sounded when we woke them up in the middle of the night. But that was the end of it.

Then, one night about a month ago, I was at home by myself. I was bored with television and tired of homework and reading and everything I could think of. I have this list of telephone numbers of a lot of the kids at school, see. So I made a couple of calls for a laugh. At first, I just joked around—like the time I called this boy whose last name is Hamm and told him my name was Eggs and I would like to have him on my plate. He didn't seem to know what to say, and I just laughed and hung up.

But things got serious the last time I made a call. I dialed this number and it was Jada's grandmother who answered the telephone. I didn't know it at the time, but Jada's grandfather was in the hospital. So I scared Jada's grandmother when I said I worked at a funeral home. I didn't mean to hurt anybody. I just wanted to have some fun.

I hear they're doing some checking now to find out who is making the calls. I don't want to get caught, so I told my friend Deidre what I had done and asked her to help me out. I want her to say that I was with her at the time the calls were made, in case somebody thinks I did it. She hasn't given me an answer yet, but I'm counting on her.

You know what it's like to be bored, don't you? I mean, you're hanging around the house with nothing to do. Or nothing you want to do. The telephone is there, so you play a few games with people. It's fun. I just shouldn't have said anything about a funeral home to Jada's grandmother. Most of the time, I say something about a pizza shop or pretend I'm selling something. I was just about to stop making the calls anyway. I hear there's a machine out now that gives your number to the person you call. But I didn't stop in time, I guess. Now I'm in trouble.

I sure hope my friend Deidre says she'll help me.

Focus on the Problem

Talk About Sheila's Actions:

1. Why is Sheila telling on herself? _____
   _____
   _____

2. Do you think she would have kept quiet if she did not think she might get caught?_____

Talk About Your Feelings:

1. Do you understand why Sheila makes these calls? _____
   _____

2. How do you feel about Sheila? _____
   _____

3. How do you feel about her having a list of other students' telephone numbers?
   _____
   _____

Talk About Sheila's Options:

1. Should Sheila tell on herself even if her friend Deidre says nothing? _____
   Explain. _____

2. Should she tell her parents? _____ Explain._____
   _____

3. Should she tell a counselor or teacher at school? _____ Explain. _____
   _____

Think and Write:

1. Write two sentences telling which option you would choose if you were Sheila and why.
   _____
   _____

2. With your partner or group, write a short role-play in which Sheila tells an adult what she has done.

3. Complete the following form for Sheila. Share it with your teacher.

I Made Crank Calls, But I Can't Tell Anybody About It

A. Based on what you know now, identify another behavior that Sheila should change. _____

_____

_____

B. Set a goal for Sheila to work toward as she makes changes. _____

_____

_____

C. Name a strategy that Sheila can use to reach her goal. _____

_____

_____

D. Tell Sheila how she can monitor her progress as she makes changes. _____

_____

_____

Signature _____ Date _____

I Know I'm Clean

As you read, consider your answer to this question:

How can students help a less-<u>fortunate</u> classmate solve some of his problems?

▶ **Pretend that Jay is a real person in your class as you read the story and complete the activities.** Jay does the best he can to be neat. He brushes his teeth most of the time, but he doesn't always have toothpaste to use. He washes each day if he can, but in cold weather it's not easy for him to take showers without hot water.

He and his brothers and sisters wash their clothes at the laundromat on the weekends when they have money. At other times, they wash their clothes at home in the sink. Jay buys and uses deodorant when he can.

Sometimes, though, he doesn't smell very good. Sometimes his breath bothers other students. His classmates make fun of him because of the way he smells and dresses. They tease him when he comes to school wearing clothes that are not quite dry.

At times, he pretends he doesn't hear the comments. At other times, he gets into fights with the students who bother him. If students tease him or laugh at him for not smelling good, he always says, "I know I'm clean."

Jay is too young to have a job. If he could work, he would buy deodorant, toothpaste, and soap regularly and have enough money for the laundromat. But what can he do now? How do you feel about the students who tease him? Would you tease him?

fortunate: lucky

Focus on the Problem

Talk About Jay:

1. What are the two problems that Jay has to solve? _____

_____

_____

2. What has Jay done to try to solve his problems? _____ Explain. _____

_____

3. How would Jay feel if his classmates treated him differently? _____
   _____

4. Will Jay have a better chance of solving his problems as he grows older? _____
   Why do you think so? _____
   _____

Talk About Jay's Options:

1. If Jay can solve his problem of not being clean, what chance is there that the second problem will go away? _____
   _____

2. Even though Jay is young, should he look for small jobs at which he could earn some money? _____

3. Do you have enough toothpaste, deodorant, and soap to share with him?_____

4. Would he accept these things if you offered them to him?_____

5. How do you think Jay would feel if you were to try to help him? _____
   _____

6. What power does Jay have to solve his own problems? _____
   _____

Talk About Your Feelings:

1. How do you feel about Jay? _____
   _____

2. How do you feel about Jay's classmates? _____
   _____

3. How do you feel about the way they treat him? _____
   _____
   _____

4. Have you ever felt that you should defend Jay or help him in some other way? _____ Explain. _____

Talk About Your Options:

1. How willing are you to confront your classmates and ask them to leave Jay alone?
   _____

2. What could you say to them that might make them listen to you? _____

   _____

3. If you were to confront them, what do you think they would say and do? _____

   _____

4. Which adult at school could you talk to about Jay and his problems? _____

   _____

5. How do you think Jay would feel if you spoke to the others about him? _____

   _____

6. What power do you have to help Jay solve his problems? _____

   _____

Take Part in a Role-Play:

You decide you are going to confront your classmates about the way they treat him. With your group, practice and present the following role-play:

You: Listen up, everybody! I called this meeting so we can talk about Jay and the way we treat him. I like Jay and I don't like what's happening to him.

Student 1: But he stinks! He's supposed to be treated like that!

Student 2: Yeah, that's right. He's dirty. I don't want to be around him. He ought to go somewhere.

Student 3: I know. And all he ever says is, "I know I'm clean." But we know he's not clean. So what are we supposed to do?

Student 4: You know, sometimes I feel sorry for Jay when everybody gives him a hard time. He lives down the street from me and he's really okay. They just have some problems at his house. He can't help it.

Student 1: But he could wash! And he could brush his teeth!

Student 4: Right. But what if he doesn't have any soap or toothpaste? His family is going through a really tough time. His pop got killed a couple of years ago, you know. Jay has a hard life.

Student 2: But you laugh at him, too. Don't try to play it off as if you don't. You don't say much, but you laugh at what everybody says.

You: All of us have laughed at the teasing once in a while. But that doesn't make it right. I'm making a promise right now. I'm not going to laugh at any more jokes or teasing. Will anybody join me?

Student 3: Are you crazy? You can't decide when people laugh and what they laugh at! I'll laugh whenever I feel like laughing! And I'll laugh at what I please!

Student 4: I'll join you. I feel bad every time I laugh at Jay. I'll feel better if I stop it.

Student 1: Well, if something is funny, I'm not going to say I won't laugh.

You: Put yourself in Jay's place. How would you feel if you were the one being laughed at?

Student 1: Please! Don't put me in his place! I don't want to be there. Ha ha. Just a little joke. Seriously, I guess you're right. I wouldn't like it if I got teased all the time. I'd probably punch somebody.

Student 4: But who would you punch? It must be pretty hard to figure out what to do when the whole class seems to be laughing at you.

You: Okay, so let's take it easy on Jay. Can we agree on that?

Student 2: All right. And you know what? I have an idea that might help Jay earn a little money to buy the stuff he needs and go to the laundromat and everything.

You: What is it?

Student 2: We could get him some jobs. You know, stuff he can do. You know how smart Jay is. He could tutor people. We could help him get together a bunch of posters and put them up in stores and some other places. He might get a lot of work that way.

You: Okay. I think he might like the idea. Let's go talk to him.

Think and Write:

1. With your group, write a different role-play for Jay and his classmates. Try hard to help Jay solve his problems. Present your role-play to the class.

2. With your classmates, complete the following form. Share it with your teacher.

I Know I'm Clean

I will work every day to treat everyone in my class with the respect that I want to get from them. I will show my respect by _____

_____

_____

_____

_____

Signature _____ Date _____

I Don't Want to Fight!

As you read, consider your answer to this question:

How can you keep from fighting when someone picks a fight with you?

 Read the story and complete the activities as though you yourself were confronting the situation. You are walking quickly down the stairs at school, thinking about getting to your next class on time. As you turn to go down the last set of stairs, you accidentally bump into another girl who is running up the stairs.

She drops her books, turns and looks at you, and says, "You better pick them up if you know what's *good* for you." She folds her arms across her chest and stares at you.

You don't think you have really done anything wrong. Bumping into her was an accident, after all. You were hurrying down the steps and she was running up the steps. So if you are guilty of anything, she's guilty of the same thing.

But you are a peaceful person, and you want to get to your next class, so you pick up her books, hand them to her, and hurry off to your next class. You get there just as the late bell rings and begin your classwork. You forget all about what happened as you go through your day.

When you leave school, you see a large group of students standing near the corner. You figure somebody must be about to fight, but you don't think much about it. As you pass the crowd, someone jumps out in front of you. When you get over your surprise, you notice it is the girl you bumped into on the stairs earlier in the day.

The crowd begins to circle around the two of you. . . .

Focus on the Problem

Talk About What Happened:

How did the other girl react when the two of you bumped into each other on the stairs? _____

_____

Talk About the Actions of the Crowd:

1. What part does the crowd play in the other girl's actions after school? _____

_____

_____

Text copyright © Anne A. Boyd and James R. Boyd. Illustrations copyright © Pearson Learning.

2. If you and the other girl do fight, who would you say is in charge of you—the girl, the crowd, or you? _____

_____

Talk About Your Actions:

1. When you picked up the girl's books from the steps, did you think there would be a problem? _____

2. Do you think it's possible that the girl is waiting for you after school *because* you picked up her books? _____

3. Do you think you are a strong-minded person? _____ How can you prove it in dealing with the problem in this scenario?_____

_____

4. Are you someone who can make up her mind and not let classmates or others change it? _____ Explain. _____

_____

Think and Write About Your Options:

1. List at least two options you had when the other girl demanded that you pick up her books.

    a. _____

    b. _____

2. What do you think would have happened if each of these options had been carried through?

    a. _____

    b. _____

3. What options do you have now that the other girl is waiting for you and you are about one minute away from a fight? _____

_____

Take Part in a Role-Play:

You look at the crowd that has gathered and decide to keep walking. You step around the crowd. The other girl throws her books to the ground and jumps in front of you. You stop walking, hold onto your books, and look at her. Finally she speaks.

The Other Girl: So, who do you think you are?

You: What are you talking about?

The Other Girl: Don't try to get smart with me. You know what I mean! You knocked my books down. Nobody knocks my books down and gets away with it.

You: That was an accident and you know it.

The Other Girl: Don't try to get out of it now. I'm going to wipe this sidewalk with you!

You: You know, I really don't have time for this nonsense. So, if you're finished, I'm going to head home on time. I have some important things to do when I get there.

The Other Girl: So, you're scared! You're scared! You know I can kick you up and down this street.

You: I'm really not scared. And maybe you can beat me. I don't know. I don't think you can. But I'll tell you one thing. You won't find out because I'm not going to fight you.

The Other Girl: Not going to fight? How can you hold your head up and walk around when you act scared like this?

You: Like I said, I'm not scared. And I can live without fighting. Why should I act like some animal and get my clothes all torn and dirty and lose my books so everybody standing around here can laugh and cheer? If you want to fight, fight some of these people who like to fight. I'm leaving. I have things to do.

A Voice in the Crowd: I thought there was going to be a fight! Why are you two just standing around?

You: You need to ask your friend here. I'm not standing around any longer. Like I said, I'm leaving.

You step around the other girl and start home. You look back once and see her staring after you. The crowd is breaking up and moving along. Just at that moment you see Officer Bennett, the school policeman, heading toward the crowd. You smile to yourself and say, half out loud, "Where were *you* five minutes ago?"

Think and Write:

1. With your partner or group write another role-play—one based on the same scenario but with a different ending. Try to think of a new ending that does not involve a fight. Practice it and present it to the class.

2. With your partner or group, complete the following form. Share it with your teacher.

I Don't Want to Fight!

A. If my classmates or I have a problem with promoting fighting, our (my) goal is to

_____

_____

B. This is a strategy that we (I) will use to reach that goal:

_____

_____

C. This is something we (I) will do to monitor our (my) behavior as changes are made: _____

_____

D. If my classmates or I have a problem with getting into fights, our (my) goal is to

_____

_____

E. This is a strategy that we (I) will use to reach that goal:

_____

_____

F. These are two things that we (I) will do to monitor our (my) behavior as changes are made:

1. _____

2. _____

Comments:

We (I) know that it may take a long time to reach our (my) goal and that we (I) may need help in doing so, but we (I) will try to finish each day without promoting or getting into a fight.

Signature _____ Date _____

Should You Take It or Leave It?

As you read, consider your answer to this question:

Why is it best to be honest?

▶ **Read the story and complete the activities as though you yourself were confronting the situation.** It's the day before your social studies report is due. You just got started on it over the weekend, and you haven't made much progress. Why did you put it off until the last minute, you wonder? Why didn't you just go ahead and get started when the work was assigned?

Mr. Sutter, your teacher, has been reminding your class every day about the importance of organizing your time and working steadily so that there would be no last-minute rush to finish. You really meant to do exactly what he asked you to do. But you just put it out of your mind because you had other things to do. And now it's due *tomorrow!*

You slowly collect your things as your classmates leave the room. By the time you get everything together, you are the last person in the room. As you walk toward the door, you glance around. You can't believe your eyes!

A classmate's neatly done report has been left on a desk. You walk over and look at it. You think about the mess you are in. There's only a slim chance you will finish your report by tomorrow. Should you return this one to the student who wrote it? Should you just leave it there? Or, what would happen if you were to take it, copy it, and hand it in?

Focus on the Problem

Talk About What Is Happening:

What are you thinking about doing? _____

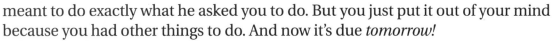

_____

Think About Your Options:

Option a

Suppose you steal the report. You take it home and copy it. The next day you hand it in to Mr. Sutter and go on your way. You try not to notice the student who is crying and trying to explain to Mr. Sutter that she really did complete her report early. You try not to hear her say that she brought it in the day before and she must have left it on her desk. You don't want to hear the tone in Mr. Sutter's voice when he reminds her of the number of times he spoke to the class about the need to plan, organize, and work day-to-day on the report. Tough luck, you think. What counts is that your report is in. You will probably get an A on it. And that's all there is to that.

Answer the Following Questions:

1. When you hand in the report, will that be the end of the story? _____

   Explain. _____

2. Even if Mr. Sutter does not find out what you did, how will stealing a report make you feel? _____

Option b

Suppose you don't take the other student's report. Instead, you hand it in to Mr. Sutter and hurry home to begin work on your report. You don't even take time out to eat dinner. You work until you fall asleep at your desk. You work on it again the next morning until you have to leave for school. You go into the restroom when you get to school to finish your title page. You are not really satisfied with your work, but at least you can hand it in on time. If you are lucky, you will get a C on it. And you promise yourself that you will never again wait until the last minute to do an assignment.

Answer the Following Questions:

1. If you choose this option, how will it make you feel? _____

   _____

2. Will you keep the promise you are making to yourself about not leaving things until the last minute? _____

   _____

Option c

Suppose you don't take the report. You just leave it where you find it and hurry home to begin work on your own report. You don't even take time out for dinner. You work until you fall asleep at your desk. But you fall asleep so early that you don't finish your assignment. You work on it again the next morning until you have to leave for school. You must make a choice. You can finish the report and hand it in without copying it. Or you can copy the part you have done and hand it in. Maybe it doesn't matter. You know you will get an F either way because it is incomplete.

Answer the Following Questions:

1. How will you feel about getting an F when you might have gotten an A, had you taken the other student's report? _____

2. Will you be glad that you were honest, even if you do fail? _____

Think and Write:

1. Would you choose Option a, or b, or c? _____ Explain your choice. _____

    _____

    _____

    _____

    _____

2. Think back to a time when you found an important item. How did you handle the situation? If you've never found an important item, think about how you would handle the situation.

    _____

    _____

    _____

    _____

    _____

    _____

3. With your classmates, complete the following form. Share it with your teacher.

Should You Take It or Leave It?

A. If my classmates or I have a problem with stealing, our (my) goal is to _____
_____
_____

B. These are two strategies that we (I) will use to reach that goal:

1. _____

2. _____

C. These are two things that we (I) will do to monitor our (my) behavior:

1. _____

2. _____

D. If my classmates or I have a problem with putting off doing assignments until the last minute, our goal is to _____
_____
_____

E. These are two strategies that we (I) will use to reach our (my) goal:

1. _____

2. _____

F. These are two things that we (I) will do to monitor our (my) behavior:

1. _____

2. _____

We will use these strategies and others for as long as it takes to reach our goal. We know that it may take a long time to make these changes, but we will work hard on them every day.

Signature _____ Date _____

Caught in the Act!

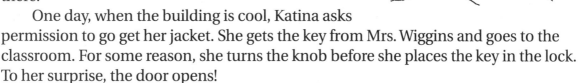

As you read, consider your answer to this question:

Why is Katina surprised to see Jared in Mrs. Wiggins's classroom?

 The school is crowded. Lockers have not yet been assigned. Students who bring jackets to school carry them from class to class. Mrs. Wiggins has a large classroom so she allows students in her homeroom to leave their jackets in the back of the room. The door to the classroom is locked when classes are not scheduled to meet there.

One day, when the building is cool, Katina asks permission to go get her jacket. She gets the key from Mrs. Wiggins and goes to the classroom. For some reason, she turns the knob before she places the key in the lock. To her surprise, the door opens!

She steps in and sees Jared going through the pockets of a jacket. He is concentrating on what he is doing and doesn't see her. She watches him place something in the pocket of his jeans. At that moment, he sees her and jumps slightly.

But he says very calmly, as he picks out his jacket, "Oh, I see you came for your jacket, too. Well, I've got mine. See you later."

Katina stares at him as he moves past her and leaves the room. She is so surprised she doesn't answer him. She looks at the key in her hand and looks at the door. Jared has said nothing about the key or the "locked" door.

Two thoughts crowd Katina's mind. For one thing, Jared has not used Mrs. Wiggins's key to enter the classroom. And for another, the jacket he is searching when Katina enters the room is not the jacket he wears when he leaves the room.

Feeling upset, Katina forgets her jacket. She carefully locks the door and heads back to the teachers' lounge to return the key to Mrs. Wiggins. On the way to the lounge, she decides not to say anything about what she has seen.

Focus on the Problem

Talk About Jared:

1. How do you think Jared got into the room?_____

_____

2. How does he react when he sees Katina?_____

_____

3. What do you think Jared put into his pocket? _____

_____

4. Does getting caught seem to bother Jared? _____

_____

5. What have you learned so far about the kind of person Jared is? _____

_____

Talk About Katina's Actions:

1. What is Katina doing in Mrs. Wiggins's classroom? _____

_____

2. How does she react when she sees Jared in the room? _____

_____

3. What does Katina think Jared took? _____

_____

4. Why do you think she is so upset? _____

_____

5. Why doesn't Katina report what she has seen? _____

_____

Talk About Katina's Options:

1. List the options you think Katina has when she sees Jared in the empty classroom.

    a: _____

    b: _____

    c: _____

2. Explain what might happen if each of these options were carried through.

    a: _____

    _____

    b: _____

    _____

    c: _____

    _____

Take Part in a Role-Play:

(Katina catches up with Jared after leaving Mrs. Wiggins's room.)

Katina: Jared, wait a minute.

Jared: What's up?

Katina: How did you get into Mrs. Wiggins's room?

Jared: I walked in. What did you expect?

Katina: You know what I mean. How did you get in without a key? I had Mrs. Wiggins's key.

Jared: Oh, now I see what you're talking about. The door was unlocked. It was closed but it wasn't locked. I guess Mrs. Wiggins is becoming a little forgetful.

Katina: She sure thought she locked the door. She gave me the key when I asked to get my jacket.

Jared: Well, you'll have to ask her about that. Like I said, maybe she forgot to lock the door. This is as far as I go. See you later.

(Jared goes into a classroom. Katina goes to the teachers' lounge.)

Katina: Mrs. Wiggins, here's your key. I didn't even get my jacket because when I opened the door, Jared surprised me. He was already in the classroom. He said the door was unlocked.

Mrs. Wiggins: He was in the classroom? Okay, Katina. I'll speak to him later. I did not give him permission to go into the room, and I know I locked the door. Thanks for telling me about this.

Think and Write:

1. One of the options you came up with earlier probably matches the events in this role-play. Decide which option it is (a, b, c) and explain the ways in which it matches the action described here.

   _____

   _____

   _____

   _____

2. Have you ever found yourself in a situation like the one Katina is in? Take a look at the monitoring form that follows Scenario 22.

It's Easy to Get Someone Else in Trouble

As you read, consider your answer to this question:

What prevents Katina from explaining her actions?

▶ Katina goes to her homeroom to get her jacket. She has gotten the key from her teacher, Mrs. Wiggins, but she finds the door already unlocked. Not only that, but she sees Jared going through the pockets of jackets in the classroom and she sees him put something in his pocket. Jared leaves the room ahead of her, taking his jacket with him. Katina locks the door without getting her jacket and goes back to the teachers' lounge to return the key to Mrs. Wiggins.

She thinks all day about what happened. She doesn't tell anyone else what she has seen. She likes Jared. Everybody thinks he's a pretty cool guy. He plays basketball and runs track. All the girls like him. She thinks she ought to talk to someone about what has happened, but she can't decide on the right person to talk to. "Oh, well," she says to herself, "I'll think about it overnight."

The next morning, Mrs. Wiggins tells Katina that the assistant principal, Mr. Farley, wants to see her. She goes to his office. He takes a note from his desk, hands it to her, and says, "Read this."

Katina can't believe what she sees. The note says, "Katina Jones took something from a jacket in homeroom. She is a thief."

Mr. Farley asks, "Were you in Mrs. Wiggins's room alone yesterday?"

"Yes. I went to get my jacket."

"Mrs. Wiggins says you did not have your jacket with you when you returned the key."

"I know. I—I forgot to get it." Katina is getting nervous. What is going on?

"You went to get your jacket but you forgot to get it," Mr. Farley says as he stares at her. "A large sum of money was taken from that room. We've got a very serious problem here, young lady. What do you have to say for yourself?"

Katina mumbles, "I—I didn't take anything. I didn't get my jacket because . . ."

Mr. Farley sits quietly, waiting for Katina to explain her actions.

Focus on the Problem

Talk About What Is Happening to Katina:

1. Name several things that happen to Katina in this scenario._____

   _____

   _____

2. What can she do to help herself?_____

   _____

Talk About Mrs. Wiggins:

1. Do you think Mrs. Wiggins knows about the missing money and the note?_____

   Why do you think this? _____

2. How do you think Mrs. Wiggins feels about Katina? _____

   _____

3. What kind of problem does Mrs. Wiggins have on her hands as a result of loaning out her key? _____

   _____

Talk About Mr. Farley:

1. Does Mr. Farley give Katina a fair chance to explain her actions? _____

2. Do you think Mr. Farley believes what is written in the note (that Katina is a thief)?_____

3. If he thinks the note is true, what does he believe about Katina? _____

   _____

4. What chance does Katina have of convincing Mr. Farley that she is telling the truth? _____

Talk About Jared:

1. What is Jared doing? _____

2. What chance is there that he will decide to tell the truth? _____

   _____

3. What is going to happen to him? _____

   _____

Text copyright © Anne A. Boyd and James R. Boyd. Illustrations copyright © Pearson Learning.

4. What should happen to him? _____

_____

5. Jared is a well-liked athlete. What difference will this fact make in the way things turn out? _____

6. Should it make a difference? _____

Give Katina Some Help:

1. Katina is having trouble speaking up for herself. Maybe if she were to write a letter to Mr. Farley, she could explain the things she can't seem to say. Write a short note telling Katina what you think she should say to Mr. Farley.

Dear Katina,

_____

_____

_____

_____

_____

_____

_____

                          Yours truly,

                    _____

2. As you further consider Katina's problem, take a look at the monitoring form that follows Scenario 22.

I Saw You Take It

As you read, consider your answer to this question:

How will Katina <u>convince</u> everyone she that has done nothing wrong?

▶ Mr. Farley, the assistant principal in Katina's school, has called her into his office. He has shown her a note that accuses her of taking some money from another student's jacket pocket. Katina knows who took the money, but she hasn't said anything about it.

"I—I didn't, I mean, I don't know anything about any money," says Katina. She can barely get the words out. She is thinking back to what happened in Mrs. Wiggins's room the day before—so that's what Jared was doing! He was stealing money! Mr. Farley is staring at her. She realizes that he has asked her a question.

"I'm sorry. I didn't hear the question. Could you repeat it?"

"Why did you go into that classroom? You say you went for your jacket, but you didn't get it. When I ask you why, you say you forgot. None of it makes any sense."

"But, I did forget," Katina says aloud, as she thinks, "Why didn't I report Jared yesterday? If I had, I wouldn't be in this mess."

Mr. Farley leaves his desk. Through the glass panel, she can see him talking with Mrs. Smith, his secretary. Mr. Farley returns to his office. He talks quietly with someone on the telephone. It sounds as if he might be talking with a counselor.

When he finishes his conversation, he turns back to Katina and says, "You ought to tell me the truth, young lady. It'll save us both a lot of time and trouble."

Slowly, Katina tells Mr. Farley all the details. When she finishes, he stares at her.

He says, "Let's just say for a moment that you are telling the truth. Why haven't you reported it before now—if not to me, at least to Mrs. Wiggins?"

"I don't know," mumbles Katina, looking down. She really doesn't know why she hasn't, and she feels a little foolish. Maybe she hasn't reported Jared because she feels some kind of *loyalty* to him. But he must have written that note, so it is clear that he feels no loyalty to her. As a matter of fact, he must not even like her very much. He knows he is getting her in trouble by blaming her for something he has done himself.

Suddenly, the door opens. Jared walks in and sits down.

"Okay," Mr. Farley says quietly. "Who took the money?"

The minute the question is asked, Jared turns to Katina. "You know you took the money," he says. "I saw you take it."

Katina cannot believe what she is hearing. She stares at Jared. Then she looks at Mr. Farley. He seems to be thinking.

Jared says again, "I saw you take it."

Mr. Farley's telephone rings. He listens for a few minutes without saying anything. At last, he says, "Thanks," and hangs up.

---

convince: make someone feel sure about something

loyalty: faithfulness

Focus on the Problem

Talk About Jared:

1. Why is Jared lying about what he has done? _____

_____

2. Is Jared taking responsibility for his actions? _____

3. Do you think Jared has thought about how his lie might be hurting Katina?

_____

4. Do you think it matters to Jared whether he hurts Katina? _____

_____

5. Is Jared likely to be kicked off the basketball and track teams if the truth comes out? _____

6. Is this perhaps the most important thing to him? _____

_____

7. Is there anything about Jared that reminds you of yourself? _____ Explain.

_____

Talk About Mr. Farley:

1. Why is he just sitting and listening to the two students? _____

_____

2. What do you think the telephone call was about? _____

_____

3. What decision is Mr. Farley going to make? _____

Talk About Katina:

1. Why doesn't Katina stand up to Jared? _____
   _____

2. Is she still hoping he will tell the truth? _____

3. Does she still want to believe in him? _____

4. Does she still think he is a "pretty cool guy"? _____

5. Why do you think Katina has trouble speaking up for herself in front of the
   principal?_____

Talk About Your Ideas:

1. How do you want this story to end? _____
   _____

2. How do you think it will end? _____
   _____

3. What do you think about what Jared is doing? _____
   _____

4. What do you think about the way Katina is handling the situation? _____
   _____

5. What do you think about the way Mr. Farley is handling things? _____
   _____

Read and Write:

Do you remember the call Mr. Farley receives while talking to Katina and Jared? It
seems Mr. Farley had asked the counselor to call Jared's parents and Katina's parents
to find out whether either student had recently spent a large amount of money.
Jared's parents report that they had given him money for new basketball shoes. They
say he bought both basketball shoes and track shoes. At the time, they wondered
about his buying two pairs of shoes, but he told them he had found a half-price sale.
After receiving the call from the counselor, Jared's parents contact the store where he
shopped and discover that there was no sale. Jared paid full price for both pairs of
shoes. He cannot explain where he got the extra money for his track shoes, and the
matter is settled.

1. Use these facts to write the last scene of the story.

2. Complete the form that follows. When you have finished, share it with your
   teacher.

Caught in the Act! (Scenario 20)

It's Easy to Get Someone Else in Trouble (Scenario 21)

and

I Saw You Take It (Scenario 22)

A. The behavior I will change is _____
_____

B. My goal is to _____
_____

C. These are two strategies I will use to reach my goal:

   1. _____
   _____

   2. _____
   _____

D. These are two things I will do to monitor my behavior as changes are made:

   1. _____
   _____

   2. _____
   _____

Signature _____ Date _____

Some of My Friends Steal, But I . . .

As you read, consider your answer to this question:

What can you do to help your friends understand that stealing is wrong?

▶ **Read the story and complete the activities as though you yourself were confronting the situation.** You meet several of your friends before school and ride the bus with them every morning. After school, you meet up with them and walk to the bus stop, which is located near a grocery store and a cart set up by a local *vendor.* That's where the problems start.

At first, it happened only once in a while. But now, almost every day, one of your friends steals something from the vendor's cart or the grocery store. Nearly everybody in the group thinks it's funny. The things they take aren't worth much money. They usually take candy bars, potato chips, gum, or popcorn—that sort of thing. What bothers you is that they have money and could buy the stuff they steal.

So far you've just pretended not to notice what is going on. You know what your friends are doing is wrong and you think you may be wrong for not saying anything to them. It's not that you're afraid to talk to them. It's just that you want to be their friend. If you say too much, they'll tell you to join in, hang around and keep your mouth shut, or get lost and let them have their fun.

You really like them. Aside from the stealing problem, they are really okay. You get along well with them. They're good friends. They just need to be told that what they're doing is wrong. What can you say or do to stop what is happening? Is talking to them going to solve the problem? Is there anybody else who can help you change the things your friends are doing?

> **vendor:** a person who sells goods

Focus on the Problem

Consider Your Options:

1. Review the two options that follow. Add others to the list.

   a: Continue to pretend not to notice what is happening.

   b: Stay away from your friends.

c: _____

d: _____

2. Think about all the options. What would happen if each of these options were carried through? How would your friendships be affected? Do you think you could make new friends if you were to lose your old ones?

I think Option a would have this effect: _____

_____

_____

I think Option b would have this effect: _____

_____

_____

I think Option c would have this effect: _____

_____

_____

I think Option d would have this effect: _____

_____

_____

Think and Write:

1. With your partner or group, choose one option. Write a short role-play in which you discuss with your classmates the issue of stealing. Use the space provided to briefly describe what you are going to write about.

_____

_____

_____

_____

2. Complete the form that follows. Sign it and share it with your teacher.

Some of My Friends Steal, But I . . .

A. The behavior I will change is _____
_____

B. My goal is to _____
_____

C. These are two strategies I will use to reach this goal:

1. _____
_____

2. _____
_____

D. These are two things I will do to monitor my behavior as changes are made:

1. _____
_____

2. _____
_____

Signature _____ Date _____

I Don't Do Drugs, But . . .

As you read, consider your answer to this question:

How can you convince your friends not to do drugs?

▶ I'm Michael Foster. I need to talk about a drug problem. No, I don't do drugs, but some of my friends do. I know they do because I've seen them use stuff on the weekends or before school. Every now and then I try to get them to stop. I tell them some of the things that my parents have told me and some of the things I've seen on television about the problems you can have if you use drugs.

But they won't listen to me and it's making me crazy. You see, I like my friends and I know they really like me. But they think they know more than they do. They think drugs don't do any harm. They say they are in control of what they do, no matter what drugs they're using. I try to tell them they can die from some of the strange pills and other junk they use. They try to tell me they can stop whenever they want to.

The problem is, I know that isn't true. I watch the way they act in school on the days when they use the stuff. Either they are sleepy and act lazy and don't want to do any work, or they act up and cause big problems in class. When I tell them what they're like in class, they tell me it's my *imagination,* but I know it isn't. They're getting a *reputation* for being troublemakers, and their grades are going down.

Except for the drugs, I like going around with my buddies. We've been friends since we were little kids. Besides, if I don't hang out with them, I won't have anybody to hang out with. I just don't want to see any of them get hurt. And I don't want to get a bad reputation—I sure don't want anybody to think I use drugs. I need help. What can I do?

---

imagination: the ability of the mind to form ideas or pictures that are not real

reputation: what people think about the kind of person someone is

---

Focus on the Problem

(As you answer these questions in the role of Michael Foster, think about your real-life friends and your school.)

Talk About Your Friends:

1. How long have your friends used drugs? _____

2. What reason do they give for using drugs? _____
   _____

3. Do their parents know about their drug use? _____
   _____

4. Have their parents talked to them about drugs? _____

5. Where do they buy the drugs they use? _____
   _____

Talk About Your School Life:

1. Does your school have a drug prevention program? _____

2. Have you been given any information about the serious problems caused by drug use? _____

Talk About Your Parents:

1. When did your parents begin to talk to you about drugs? _____
   _____

2. What did they do or say to convince you not to use drugs? _____
   _____

3. Do you think your parents would talk to your friends about drugs? _____

4. Would your friends listen to them? _____

Talk About a Plan of Action:

1. You have been told that getting reliable information out to your friends is the best thing to do in this situation. Where will you get that information? _____
   _____

2. Once you have it, how will you get it out to your classmates and friends? _____
   _____

3. Do you think your friends will accept what you have to say if you have new information to offer them? _____ Explain. _____

_____

_____

Read and Write:

1. In an effort to reach his friends, Michael decides to write a letter to his counselor requesting her help in putting together information on the dangers of drug use. What do you think of Michael's approach?

_____

_____

_____

Dear Ms. Black,

    I'm writing to ask you if I can join you in thinking of ways to convince some of the students to stop using drugs. I'm not trying to tell on anybody. I just want to help kids stop. Sometimes I talk to them, but they tell me I don't know what I'm talking about. I know a lot about drugs because my parents have talked to me about the harm they can do.

    I think kids might stop using drugs if they had good information about the effects of drugs on their bodies. They need information from experts—maybe they would believe them. They need more than what's written in our textbooks because sometimes they don't want to pay attention to what they find only in their books.

    Do you have any videos or movies or anything like that? Could we make a video? Maybe some of the local groups that tell kids to stay away from drugs would come to our school. I'll bet the whole school would listen to a pro quarterback or basketball player or a golfer. Could we get somebody like that? Maybe Michael Jordan or Tiger Woods (Just kidding.)?

    Anyway, I want to help work on this problem. But don't tell anybody I wrote you.

Yours truly,
Michael Foster

2. Complete the following form. Share it with your teacher when you are finished.

I Don't Do Drugs, But . . .

A. The behavior I will change is _____

_____

Desired goals (choose one):

Learn about the dangers of drug use

Remain drug free

Help friends to be drug free

B. My goal is to _____

_____

C. These are two strategies I will use to reach my goal:

1. _____

_____

2. _____

_____

D. While I work to reach my goal, I will monitor my behavior by doing the following:

1. _____

_____

2. _____

_____

E. My target date for reaching my goal is _____

F. I have _____ to work on reaching my goal behavior.
      (How many days, weeks?)

Signature _____ Date _____

How Much Did Your Sneakers Cost?

As you read, consider your answer to this question:

Why are some students so concerned about how much things cost?

Sharon and her brother Sean are lucky in many ways. They live with both their parents in a beautiful house; they have friends; they are above-average students. They get almost everything they want, including name-brand clothes and sneakers. Sean gets a haircut before he even needs one, and Sharon has her hair and nails done every week.

They both have one big problem, though. They feel that it's okay to tease other students who don't have what they have. They laugh at the way some of their class-mates dress. They accuse other students of not smelling good. They want to know how much everybody's sneakers cost. If it's a small amount, they laugh.

Sharon teases other girls about their hair and fingernails. Sean embarrasses some of the boys in his class by making them show the tags in their shirts to prove

they are wearing brand-name clothes. They both make fun of anyone who is not wearing expensive things.

The other students are *intimidated* by Sean and Sharon. From time to time, someone threatens to "deal with" them, but that causes more teasing. They don't see anything wrong with the things they say. Maybe they think what they say and do is okay because when they pick on a student, many of their classmates join them in laughing at the other student. Why do Scan and Sharon do what they do? What can be done to stop them?

intimidated: bullied; made afraid

Focus on the Problem

Talk About the Actions of Sean and Sharon:

1. Why do you think Sean and Sharon do the things they do? _____

_____

_____

2. Do you think anyone has ever tried to talk to them about their behavior? _____
Why or why not?_____

_____

Talk About the Actions of their Classmates:

1. How are the students whom Sean and Sharon are picking on being affected?

_____

2. How is the bullying affecting the class as a whole? _____

_____

3. Are Sean and Sharon's classmates helping to promote the teasing? _____
Explain. _____

_____

_____

_____

4. Do the other students really think what Sean and Sharon are doing is funny?
_____ Explain. _____

Talk About Your Feelings and Actions:

1. Are there any students like Sean and Sharon in your classes? _____
2. If so, how do you feel about these students?_____

_____

3. Have they ever teased you? _____

_____

4. Will you go out of your way to be nice to these students so they won't tease you?

_____

5. Do you ever tease other students? _____ Why or why not?_____

_____

6. If you do tease others, does it make you feel more important or "cooler" than
those you tease? _____

7. Do you believe you don't look okay unless some of your classmates say you do?

_____

8. Do you think any student has the right to criticize the way another student
dresses? _____ Explain. _____

Talk About Options for the Class:

With your partner or group, consider these and other ways to stop Sean and Sharon from bothering other students. Discuss all options.

1. An adult could be asked to help solve the problem. _____

    _____

2. A meeting could be held among the students to discuss Sean and Sharon's actions, either

    a. Without Sean and Sharon present_____

    b. With Sean and Sharon present_____

3. Sean and Sharon's classmates could agree to stop listening to the things the two say. _____

Take Part in a Short Role-Play:

(The following scene takes place in Sean and Sharon's classroom.)

Sean: Hey, man! Where did you find those sneakers? In a homeless shelter? That must be where they came from because they sure look down and out. (The class laughs.)

Student A: Sean, why don't you leave people alone? What makes you think you have the right to talk about people the way you do?

Sean: I'm not bothering you, am I? Mind your business. I'm talking to my buddy here.

Student B: Don't call me your buddy. I'm not your buddy. You bug me. All you ever do is talk about people. Who do you think you are?

Sean: I'm somebody who can talk about you and your high-water pants and dingy old socks.

(Some students laugh.)

Student A: Sean, people have really gotten tired of the way you treat everybody. You think you have some special right to say anything you want, just because you wear nice clothes. Your clothes don't mean that much to me.

Sean: Yes, they do. You know they do. All of you wish you had what I have.

(The late bell rings and the teacher enters the classroom. The conversation stops.)

Think and Write:

1. With your partner or group, finish writing this role-play. When you're finished, choose roles and act it out.

2. Complete the Goals, Strategies, and Monitoring form that follows Scenario 26.

If I Could Just Shut Him Up!

As you read, consider your answer to this question:

How can you help an annoying classmate change his behavior without getting into a fight with him?

Yo! My name's Mark. I'm one of the students in a lot of Sean's classes. He thinks he is somebody special. I mean, I know we are all special, but he takes it too far. His mom and pop both have good jobs. They have a nice crib and he wears some decent threads, but that doesn't give him the right to "bust on" people just because they don't have what he has. Most of the people in class just laugh at what he says. I don't think they always agree with him. I think they want to tell him to stop. But no one ever says anything.

Sometimes, when he starts bothering somebody, I just want to get up and punch him out. I'm not afraid of him, so I would do it, but I'm already on probation. If I do anything else right now I'll really be in trouble. And besides, I'm working on managing my behavior better. I have been learning to search for positive options instead of doing the same old negative things I always used to do. I don't succeed every time, which is why I'm on probation, but I am trying.

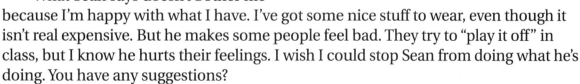

Anyway, it just doesn't seem fair that Sean gets all that expensive stuff and he's still not happy until he bothers somebody else about what they don't have. I think he's got some kind of problem that he's not dealing with. My folks tell me it doesn't matter what you put on the outside of you if there is something wrong with what's on the inside.

What Sean says doesn't bother me because I'm happy with what I have. I've got some nice stuff to wear, even though it isn't real expensive. But he makes some people feel bad. They try to "play it off" in class, but I know he hurts their feelings. I wish I could stop Sean from doing what he's doing. You have any suggestions?

Focus on the Problem

Consider Mark's Options:

1. Discuss this list of actions that Mark (or another student) could take to stop Sean from making fun of other students in the class. **Note:** Actions that could get a student in trouble, such as punching or fighting, have been left out.

a. Talk to Sean and Sharon in the classroom, on the way home, in the lunchroom, on the telephone, in a signed note.

b. Ask a favorite teacher for help.

c. Ask his parents to talk to Sean and Sharon's parents.

d. Organize the class; convince classmates to stop laughing at the things Sean and Sharon say.

e. Quietly speak out for other students who don't defend themselves.

2. Complete the following form for Sean (and yourself, if you do the things he does).

How Much Did Your Sneakers Cost? (Scenario 25)
and
If I Could Just Shut Him Up!
(Scenario 26)

A. 1. Identify a behavior that Sean should change. _____

_____

_____

2. Set a goal for Sean to aim for as he makes changes. _____

_____

3. Name two strategies that Sean can use to reach his goal.

a. _____

b. _____

4. Name two things that Sean can do to monitor his progress as he makes changes in his behavior.

a. _____

b. _____

B. 1. The behavior I am going to change is _____

_____

2. The goal I am going to work toward as I make changes is _____

_____

3. The strategy I will use to reach my goal is _____

_____

_____

4. I will monitor my progress as I make changes in my behavior by _____

_____

_____

Signature _____ Date _____

Is It Ever Okay to Lie?

As you read, consider your answer to this question:

Can a lie be helpful or positive in some way?

▶ Jack and Thomas dance around each other like a pair of boxers. As they *spar,* the crowd around them grows and the noise gets louder. A few punches are exchanged.

"Back off, man, before I punch you out!" yells Thomas.

"Yeah, come on, let's see what you can do!" challenges Jack.

At this point, Martin, who is president of the student body and a good friend of both Jack and Thomas, steps forward: "Okay, you guys. Why don't you cool it? You know what the rules are. You're just going to get yourselves in some big trouble. Come on. Let's go to class."

Mr. Farley, the assistant principal, turns the corner and sees the group of students. When they see him, they begin to move down the hall away from him. He *recognizes* Martin and calls to him: "Martin! What was that all about?"

"Oh, nothing much," replies Martin. "Somebody slipped and fell and when he didn't get up right away, they thought maybe he was hurt. But he was okay."

As Martin heads to his next class, he thinks about the new rule he and the other student council members have just helped the school to *adopt.* The rule states clearly that there is to be no fighting. Any student who is caught fighting is subject to immediate suspension. Martin thinks it is a good rule. It has cut down on the number of fights so far.

Then he thinks about his friends, Jack and Thomas, and wonders what they could have been thinking. They both know that if they are suspended, they are *automatically* dropped from any sports teams they are on. Both boys are good athletes. By his actions, Martin has saved them from suspension. But he wonders to himself, "Did I do the right thing? Suppose they decide to fight anyway? Could I get myself in trouble by trying to cover for them?"

What do you think? Did Martin do the right thing? How about you—have you ever lied to help someone?

---

adopt: to take and use as one's own
automatically: done without thinking

recognize: to know by a certain feature
spar: to box in a skillful and careful way

Focus on the Problem

Talk About Martin:

1. Was Martin doing his job as student body president when he stopped the fight? _____ Explain. _____

2. Do you think he was doing his job when he lied to the assistant principal? _____ Explain. _____

Talk About Your Feelings:

1. How do you feel about what Martin did? _____

_____

2. Do you feel that Martin's actions could cause a problem larger than the three boys themselves? _____ Explain why or why not. _____

_____

3. If a person tells a lie to help someone else, is it the same as if the person lies to help himself? _____ Explain. _____

_____

Talk About Your Actions:

1. Have you ever lied to protect yourself? _____

If yes, describe what happened. _____

_____

_____

2. Have you ever lied to help someone else? _____

If yes, describe what happened. _____

_____

Think and Write:

1. With your partner or group, write a follow-up scenario based on one of the following:

   a. Either Jack or Thomas thanks Martin for his help.

   b. Jack and Thomas fight again at a later time. Mr. Farley finds out that Martin stopped them earlier.

   c. Martin thinks about what he has done and decides he should report himself.

2. Complete the following form. Share it with your teacher.

Is It Ever Okay to Lie?

A. 1. Identify a behavior that you think Martin should change. _____

_____

_____

2. Set a goal for Martin to aim for as he makes changes. _____

_____

_____

3. Name a strategy that he can use to reach his goal. _____

_____

_____

4. Explain how he can monitor his progress as he makes changes in his behavior.

_____

_____

B. 1. The behavior I am going to change is _____

_____

2. The goal I am going to work toward as I make changes is_____

_____

3. The strategy I will use to reach my goal is _____

_____

4. I will monitor my progress as I make changes in my behavior by _____

_____

_____

Signature _____ Date _____

Has Anyone Ever "Pushed Your Buttons"?

As you read, consider your answer to this question:

Are there certain things that someone can say to you that will always cause you to react?

Read the story and complete the activities as though you yourself were confronting the situation.

A. You have had an extremely good day in school so far. You are working on a composition in class. Everything is calm and quiet. Suddenly you hear someone whisper your name. You glance around the room. Everyone is working steadily. You go back to your work. In a few minutes, you hear your name being whispered again. You look up, feeling angry now.

You settle back into your work. Once again, you hear your name whispered. That's it! Someone is purposely annoying you by whispering your name. You are not going to take this anymore. You cannot stand to hear anyone whisper your name. Everyone knows this. You decide it must be the guy behind you since no one else seems to have heard anything.

You make up your mind. The next time it happens, you are going to teach him a lesson. You don't care what happens after that. What he is doing is wrong and he's not going to get away with it. You hear your name once more. You jump up and—WHAM!

B. It's another day in school. You and your classmates are working on a project in small groups. Somebody in your group laughs aloud. The teacher calls your name and tells you to stop. It really wasn't you who laughed, but you say nothing.

There is another outburst of laughter from someone in your group. To the person who is laughing out loud, you say, "Cool it, man."

Once again, the teacher calls your name and tells you to stop it, "I know it's you. . . . You are always causing a problem."

You try to explain, but the teacher won't listen. You have had it. Nobody accuses you of something you did not do. If it happens again, you are going to. . . .

It happens again.

"push your buttons": do or say something that will always cause you to react negatively

Focus on the Problem

Talk About What Has Happened:

1. In Story A, what takes place? _____

_____

_____

2. In Story B, what takes place? _____

_____

_____

Talk About What Will Happen Next:

1. In Story A, what will happen next? _____

_____

_____

2. In Story B, what will happen next? _____

_____

_____

3. In each case, has someone's "button been pushed"? _____

4. How could all of this have been prevented? _____

_____

Talk About the Actions of the Other Students in Story A:

1. In Story A, why do you suppose the student is whispering your name? _____

_____

2. Is the student really annoying you that much by saying your name?_____

3. Has the student touched you or harmed you in some way? _____

_____

Talk About the Teacher's Actions in Story B:

1. In Story B, what is the teacher doing that is upsetting you?_____

_____

2. What might have happened if you had spoken up when the problem started?

_____

3. What do you expect the teacher to do now? _____

Talk About Your Reactions in Real Life:

1. Do you have any "hot buttons"? _____

2. Without revealing what they are, try to estimate how often they are "pushed."

   _____

3. Have your partner or group try to figure out what your "hot button" issues are. List them here: _____

4. Why are these issues important to you? _____

   _____

5. Do others see them as being important to you? _____

   _____

6. Do the issues seem to matter as much when you talk to others about them?

   _____

7. Do you think you will ever reach a point where you no longer react when some-one pushes your buttons? _____

Talk About Solutions to the Problem:

1. What are some things you can do to stop yourself from reacting to the actions of others? _____

2. How do you react when the teacher says something you don't like? _____

   _____

3. What could you say to the teacher to explain your actions and register your concern? _____

Think and Write:

1. Explain what is meant by the following: "If you always react to statements by others, then you are not really in charge of yourself." _____

   _____

   _____

2. Complete the form that follows. Share it with your teacher.

Has Anyone Ever "Pushed Your Buttons"?

A. The behavior I will change is _____

_____

B. My goal is to _____

_____

C. The strategy I will use to reach my goal is _____

_____

_____

D. While I work to reach my goal, I will monitor my progress by _____

_____

_____

E. My target date for reaching my goal is _____

Signature _____ Date _____

Taking Responsibility for Your Actions, Part 1

As you read, consider your answer to this question:

Who is really responsible for what happens to Roz?

▶ Jan and her younger sister Roz fight a lot. They fight about their clothes; they fight about cleaning the large bedroom they share; they fight about their other chores; they fight about who picks the TV shows they watch. Usually Jan starts the fights. Both girls have been told by their parents that a severe punishment awaits them the next time they fight.

Jan and Roz's parents go out for the evening. Soon after they leave, Jan and Roz begin to argue about who is going to do the dishes. In a few minutes, they begin to fight. They are in the kitchen. As they fight, Jan's arm hits the handle of a pot on the stove. The hot spaghetti sauce spills on Roz. Her arm is badly burned.

They dial 911 and Roz is rushed to the hospital. On the way, Jan tells Roz that they are going to tell their parents that it was just an accident. Roz is not to say anything about the fighting. "Besides," Jan says to her sister, "if you had just gone ahead and washed the dishes like I told you to, none of this would have happened."

Focus on the Problem

Talk About Jan:

1. What kind of person does Jan seem to be? _____
_____

2. Is she taking responsibility for what she has done? _____
_____

Talk About Roz:

1. Why do you think Roz allows Jan to treat her the way she does?_____
_____

129

2. Is Roz at all responsible for what happens?_____

_____

Relate This Event to Your School Life:

1. Do you know any students who try to control others the way Jan does Roz?

_____

2. How do you feel about these students? _____

3. Do these students seem to think that what they are doing is wrong, or do they think their actions are OK? _____

Take Part in Two Role-Plays:

Role-Play I

(Jan and Roz are on the way to the hospital.)

Jan: You'd better not tell Mom and Dad what happened! Just tell them you walked past the stove and your sleeve got caught.

Roz: My arm hurts! You made me hurt my arm! (She cries.)

Jan: Well, you ought to do what I tell you to do. Then your arm wouldn't be hurt. All you had to do was wash the dishes. You didn't have anything else to do.

Roz: But Mommy told you to clean up the kitchen. You were supposed to wash the dishes. My arm hurts.

Jan: I'm sorry you got burned. But you'd better not tell on me. If you do, you'll be sorry. Like I said, there wouldn't be a problem if you had just done what I said.

Roz: *(Crying.)* My arm hurts! What makes you think I always have to do what you say? It's not fair.

Jan: That's the way things are. I'm older than you, so I'm in charge of you. And don't you forget it.

Roz: That's not what Mom said. You're going to get in trouble. I'm going to tell her just what happened.

Jan: I'm warning you! Just try it.

Roz: I'm going to tell because you always try to blame me when you do something wrong. And I'm going to tell because my arm hurts.

Jan: Well, suit yourself. It's my word against yours. We'll see who wins.

Role-Play 2

(Jan and Roz are on the way to the hospital.)

Jan: Roz, I'm really sorry you got burned. It was my fault. If I had just washed the dishes like Mom told me to, you wouldn't be hurt. I'm sorry.

Roz: I know you wouldn't try to burn me on purpose. But what do we tell Mom and Dad?

Jan: We'll just tell them the truth. We'll tell them we were fighting about doing the dishes.

Roz: But you'll get in trouble. Big trouble.

Jan: I know.

Roz: I can just say I bumped into the pot by accident.

Jan: No. It was my fault. Mom's been telling me I would have problems if I didn't make some changes. I guess something like this had to happen to help me understand what she was saying.

Roz: Are you sure you want to do that?

Jan: Yeah, I'll tell the truth and take my punishment. By getting burned, you're already getting punishment you don't deserve. But I'll make it up to you. Things are going to be different. You'll see.

Roz: Okay. My arm does hurt.

Jan: I'm really sorry.

Talk Again About Jan and Roz:

1. How is Jan different in the two role-plays? _____

   _____

   _____

   _____

2. In the second role-play, why do you think Roz is willing to make excuses for Jan?

   _____

   _____

3. Complete the "Goals, Strategies, and Monitoring" form that follows Scenario 31.

Taking Responsibility for Your Actions, Part 2

As you read, consider your answer to this question:

Why would one student throw a tack at another student during class?

 Mrs. French, the math teacher, has assigned the class a trick problem. The person who solves it first gets a prize. Everyone is working hard to find a solution to the problem. Suddenly, Jason yells, "Ouch! Who did that?"

He grabs the back of his head. There is a tiny speck of blood on his hand. Mrs. French tries to find out what has happened. It seems someone has thrown a tack or other sharp item with such force that it made a tiny cut on Jason's head. There are four students sitting behind Jason. Any one of them might be guilty.

Mrs. French says, "Okay. Who did it? It had to be one of the four of you, because you are the only ones back there. We've talked about taking responsibility for our actions. I'd really like to settle this issue now."

"I didn't do it," says Josh.

"Wasn't me," says Craig.

"I was doing my work," declares Jada.

"I don't even know what happened," claims Roger.

Focus on the Problem

Talk About the Guilty Student:

1. Will the guilty person confess? _____ Why or why not? _____

   _____

2. Do you think you might know who the guilty person might be? _____

   Explain. _____

   _____

Talk About the Other Students:

1. Should students sitting nearby tell the teacher who is guilty? _____ Why or why not? _____

2. What will happen if someone tells the teacher? _____

_____

Think and Write:

1. Write about a time when you did something wrong in school and failed to take responsibility for it. _____

_____

2. Write about a time when you did something wrong in school and did take responsibility for it. _____

_____

Take Part in Two Role-Plays:

Role-Play I

Mrs. French: We have to get this settled immediately. Who threw the tack? *(She listens for a moment, but no one says anything.)* Nobody. Well, we'll get to the bottom of this, I can assure you. Jason, I'm sorry this happened. But I'll take care of it. Here's a pass to the nurse so she can take a look at your head. Okay, Josh, did you throw the tack?

Josh: No! Why are you always accusing me?

Mrs. French: I'm not accusing you. I'm simply trying to find out what happened. Craig, did you do it?

Craig: No.

Mrs. French: Jada, did you throw the tack?

Jada: No, I did not!

Roger: Don't even ask me! I didn't do it. And I don't want to hear anything else about it. You get on my nerves. Jason gets on my nerves! Get out of my face! I didn't do anything!

Mrs. French: Well, we won't waste any more class time on this. I'm going to have a conference with each of you about it. I'm sorry that three innocent people have to be involved. But I'll settle it as quickly as I can.

Roger: I'm not staying for any conference, and you can't make me!

Role-Play 2

Mrs. French: We have to get this matter settled. Who threw the tack? *(She listens for a moment, but no one says anything.)* Nobody? Well, we'll get to the bottom of this one way or another. Jason, I'm sorry this happened. But I'll take care of it. Here's a pass to the nurse so she can take a look at your head. Josh, did you throw the tack?

Josh: No! Why are you always accusing me?

Mrs. French: I'm not accusing you. I'm just trying to find out what happened. Craig, did you do it?

Craig: No.

Mrs. French: Jada, did you throw the tack?

Jada: No, I did not!

Mrs. French: Roger, did you throw the tack?

Roger: Yes. I might as well admit it.

Mrs. French: Why would you do such a thing? It was dangerous as well as disruptive.

Roger: I don't know. I saw the tack and I just did it. Besides, I don't like Jason. He gets on my nerves. He kept saying he was going to win the prize. I just wanted to stop him. I didn't think it would hurt him.

Mrs. French: I appreciate your being honest, Roger. What you did was wrong, though. Stay with me when the class leaves. There will be a consequence for you. Okay, class, let's get back to work.

Talk About the Characters:

1. What reason did Roger give for his actions? _____

2. What consequence should Roger suffer for throwing the tack? _____

   _____

3. Complete the "Goals, Strategies, and Monitoring" form that follows Scenario 31.

Taking Responsibility for Your Actions, Part 3

As you read, consider your answer to this question:

Who is responsible for the serious problem that arises?

▶ One day a few months ago, Jim's Aunt Sadie let him drive her car around the block as a special treat. They were in the car together that day when Jim began pestering her to let him get behind the wheel. She said, "I really shouldn't do this. If anything were to happen, I'd be in trouble with my insurance company." But Jim begged her and she finally gave in.

From that time on, Jim was hooked on driving. Jim and his friend Alex began "borrowing" his Aunt Sadie's car after school and riding around in it. Neither Jim nor Alex has a driver's license. In fact, they are too young to have a driver's license, but they both say they know how to drive.

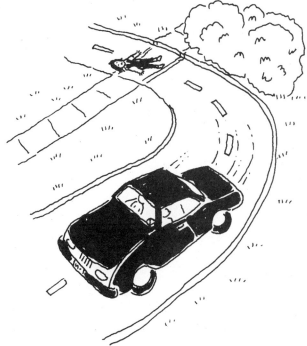

Aunt Sadie uses public transportation to go to work. On some days after work, she goes to her college classes and doesn't get home until very late. On one of her late days, Jim and Alex get into her car to do a little riding around. Alex is driving. He is driving faster than he should. As he turns a corner, little Tracey is crossing the street to go to the candy store. Alex hits her. He is scared and speeds away.

Alex finally stops the car a few miles away. The boys break a window, and pull a few wires from around the **ignition.** They leave the car and walk home. They decide they will not say anything about what has happened. If it comes up, they will suggest that the car was probably stolen. They do not mention Tracey.

> **ignition:** the electrical system that starts a car

Focus on the Problem

Talk About Jim and Alex:

1. What kind of person do you think Jim is? _____

_____

2. What do you think about Alex? _____

_____

3. Can Jim and Alex fairly say that Jim's Aunt Sadie shares in the blame for what
happened? _____ Explain _____.

_____

4. Why didn't Jim and Alex stop to check on Tracey? _____

_____

Talk About Your Feelings:

1. If you knew Jim and Alex, if they were friends or classmates, how would you feel
about them? _____

2. What do you think of someone who wouldn't stop to check on a child whom he
or she hit while driving? _____

3. Of all the things the boys did wrong, which do you feel is the worst?_____
Why?_____

_____

4. Do you think that there is something the boys can do to make up for the harm
they have done? _____

Talk About What Should Happen:

1. What two things should Jim and Alex do at once? _____

_____

2. Do you think that they will do either of these things? _____ Why or why not?

_____

_____

3. Can you think of anything Aunt Sadie could or should do? _____

_____

4. Even if Tracey is not badly hurt, should Jim and Alex be arrested? _____
Explain. _____

5. If so, what should the boys be charged with? _____

_____

Talk About What Could Happen:

Pretend that you are a friend of Jim and Alex. On the morning after the accident, they tell you what happened. They want you to help them. The first thing they do is ask you about Tracey. You tell them you have heard she is all right, except for some bumps and scratches. Then they ask you to help them find a way to talk to Aunt Sadie and the police and anybody else they should approach. What would you suggest they do?

_____

_____

_____

_____

Review of Scenarios 29, 30, and 31

Think and Write:

1. Write one sentence summing up what you think about Jan in Scenario 29.

   _____

   _____

2. Write one sentence summing up what you think about Roger in Scenario 30.

   _____

   _____

3. Write one sentence summing up what you think about Jim and Alex in Scenario 31. _____

   _____

4. Scenario 29 takes place in someone's home. Scenario 30 takes place in school. Scenario 31 takes place in the neighborhood. In all the stories, however, the main characters have something in common. What is it? _____

   _____

5. Choose a character from Scenario 29, 30, or 31 (Jan, Roz, Jim, or Alex) and complete the following form for that character. Then complete the form for yourself.

Taking Responsibility for Your Actions

A. 1. Identify a behavior that _____ should change. _____
(Name)

_____

2. Set a goal for this character as he or she makes changes. _____

_____

3. Name a strategy that this character can use to reach his or her goal. _____

_____

_____

4. Tell this character how to monitor his or her progress as changes are made.

_____

_____

B. 1. Identify a behavior that you should change. _____

2. Set a goal for yourself as you make changes. _____

_____

3. Name a strategy that you can use to reach your goal. _____

_____

_____

4. Describe how you will monitor your progress as you make changes._____

_____

_____

Signature _____ Date _____

Why Is Everybody Looking at Me?

As you read, consider your answer to this question:

How can one seemingly small action by one student disrupt an entire class?

A. Salina walks into the classroom a few minutes late and slams the door behind her. The other students look at her as she heads toward her seat. She yells, "Why is everybody looking at me?"

No one says anything to her. Mrs. Jamison, the teacher, makes a note in her rollbook. After a few instructions, the class begins to break into groups. The students locate their seats by checking group-assignment slips that the teacher had given them earlier. There are just enough students to form five groups—except for Salina, who has not yet gotten her group assignment from the teacher. As Mrs. Jamison heads in her direction, Salina snatches a slip from another student. The teacher tells Salina that she is about to hand her an assignment slip.

Salina yells, "I don't want that one. I want the one I have!" The other students all look at her. She yells, "Why is everybody looking at me?" She pushes the other student.

Mrs. Jamison tells Salina that her behavior is unacceptable. She compliments the student who has been pushed by Salina because the student does not strike back. She asks the class to begin the assignment and excuse her while she talks to Salina.

"What's wrong, Salina?" asks Mrs. Jamison.

"They're looking at me!" Salina shouts.

Again, the students look at her. She runs from the room, shouting, "Stop looking at me! Stop looking at me!"

B. It's Monday morning. Classes are just getting started. In Mr. Frye's room, students are handing in homework and getting settled. Mr. Frye is taking attendance.

Suddenly, the door bursts open. Raymond walks in, slams the door shut, and starts talking to someone across the room. Everyone is surprised. They all look at Raymond. Raymond glares back at them and yells, "Why is everybody looking at me?"

Focus on the Problem

Talk About the Class:

1. In both Story A and Story B, the same thing is happening in the classroom. What is it? _____

2. How do the other students react to the disruptive behaviors of Salina and Raymond? _____

   _____

3. How does the teacher respond to Salina? _____

   _____

Talk About Salina:

1. What do you think Salina's problem is? _____

   _____

2. Is she disrupting the class on purpose? _____ Explain. _____

   _____

3. What part do the other students play in what Salina does? _____

   _____

4. How do you think behavior such as Salina's should be handled? _____

   _____

Talk About Raymond:

1. What do you think Raymond's problem is?_____

   _____

2. Is he disrupting the class on purpose? _____ Explain._____

   _____

3. What part do the other students play in what he does? _____

   _____

4. How do you think behavior such as Raymond's should be handled?_____

   _____

Talk About Yourself:

1. How do you feel when other students disrupt your class the way Salina and Raymond do theirs?_____

   _____

2. Do you ever do things to disrupt any of your classes? Answer honestly. _____

   _____

3. Explain the harm done to everyone when one student behaves in a disruptive
   manner. _____

Talk About Your Class:

1. Do your classmates join in when
   someone disrupts the class? _____

   _____

   _____

   _____

2. Do you think your classmates ever
   wish the disruptive behavior would
   stop but are afraid to admit it? _____

   _____

   _____

   _____

Make Some Suggestions for Change:

1. Discuss these suggestions for ending disruption in your classes; add other ideas
   as well.

   a. always refuse to join in class disruptions

   b. try to convince friends not to join in class disruptions

   c. let disruptive students know you want to learn, not waste time on their antics

   d. model acceptable behavior for your classmates

   e. (other idea) _____

   f. (other idea) _____

2. Complete the following form. Share it with your teacher.

Goals, Strategies, and Monitoring Form 32

Why Is Everybody Looking at Me?

A. The behavior I will change is ______________________________

____

B. My goal is to ______________________________

____

C. The strategy I will use for reaching my goal is ______________________________

____

____

D. While I work to reach my goal, I will monitor my progress by ______________________________

____

____

Signature ______________________________ Date ______________

Yo, Dude! What's Up?

As you read, consider your answer to this question:

What causes an otherwise good student to behave in a thoughtless manner?

▶ The late bell has rung. The hallway is clear and classes have started. Students are listening as the teacher explains the day's lesson. Suddenly, a figure appears in the doorway. Earl, who is late for his class next door, yells to his buddy, Nathan.

"Yo, dude, what's up?"

At this point, the class stops working and stares at Earl. The students laugh.

Sarah yells at Earl, "Get out of here, boy, and leave us alone!" Earl slams the door after making faces at Sarah.

Sarah is now angry and Nathan is embarrassed. The class has been disrupted. The teacher is angry. Students are talking and laughing. Sarah is thinking aloud about what she will do to Earl when she has the chance. Nathan just wishes the whole thing hadn't happened in the first place. Why would Earl think it is acceptable to create such a problem in a friend's classroom?

Focus on the Problem

Talk About Earl's Behavior:

1. Why do you think Earl yells into the classroom? _____

2. Do you believe he thought before he acted? _____ Explain._____

   _____

3. Do you believe Earl thinks what he did is acceptable? _____

4. Does it seem to bother him that he has upset an entire class? _____

Talk About the Class's Reaction:

1. What do you think about Sarah's reaction? _____

   _____

2. Does she make the problem worse? _____ Explain. _____

_____

_____

3. Is it possible for someone to make a problem worse by trying to be helpful? _____ Explain, in terms of this scenario. _____

_____

_____

4. What do you think about Nathan's reaction? Is it what you would have expected?

_____

5. Why does the class join in the confusion? _____

_____

Talk About Your Feelings:

1. How do you feel when your class is interrupted by someone's silly actions?

_____

2. Do you feel that there are ways in which you and the other students can help prevent problems such as the one Earl creates? _____

_____

3. How would you feel if you were the person Earl spoke to? _____

Talk About Your Class:

1. Do you think your class is generally well behaved? _____ Why do you feel this way? _____

2. Are there many students in class who want to avoid disruptions so learning can take place? _____ Explain. _____

3. What do you think your teacher can do to handle disruptive students like Earl and promote learning? _____

_____

4. See the combined monitoring form for Scenarios 33 and 34 after Scenario 34.

What Did I Do?

As you read, consider your answer to this question:

Why won't Earl admit that he is wrong for yelling into a classroom?

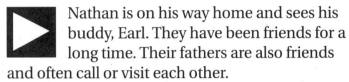

▶ Nathan is on his way home and sees his buddy, Earl. They have been friends for a long time. Their fathers are also friends and often call or visit each other.

Nathan asks Earl, "Man, why did you do what you did this morning?"

"Do what? What did I do?" Earl looks puzzled.

Nathan says, "Oh, come on, man. You know I'm talking about yelling into my classroom."

"Oh, that," Earl laughs. "I was just having a little fun. Anyway, I was speaking to you."

"Well, I don't want you to speak to me like that again. You embarrassed me and you also upset the class."

Earl replies, "Oh, no big thing."

"It was a big thing! We didn't even have class after you yelled in the door, man. You made Sarah angry and she never did shut up. And we had a class meeting to talk about ways to cut down on class confusion. You blew it when you yelled in that door."

"I didn't mean to cause a problem," Earl said. "Like I told you, I was just having a little fun."

"As far as I'm concerned, that's a strange way to have fun. It doesn't make any sense to me. You walk by that classroom door every day and you've never yelled in before. Why'd you do it today?"

"I don't know. I just thought of it and I did it. Give me a break."

Nathan asks Earl, "What do you plan on saying to your parents if the teacher calls your house and tells your dad what you did? And suppose my dad asks me about it. What am I supposed to say?

"Just say I didn't do it."

"You're expecting me to lie?" asks Nathan. "After the way you messed up my class and embarrassed me?"

"Hey, man. I am your buddy. Give me a break."

"I'll tell you what I'm going to do," Nathan answers. "I won't say anything. But if it happens again, I'm not going to hold back. And if my folks press me about it this time, I'm going to tell them exactly what happened.

Focus on the Problem

Talk About Earl:

1. Does Earl seem to be bothered by what he has done? _____

   _____

2. How does he explain his actions? _____

   _____

3. Does he seem to understand what a big problem he created? _____

   _____

4. Is he more concerned about Nathan and the other students or himself? _____

   Explain. _____

5. What kind of student would you say Earl is? _____

   _____

Talk About Nathan:

1. Does Nathan seem to be a good student or a playful one? _____

   Explain your answer. _____

2. What does Nathan tell Earl? _____

   _____

   How does Nathan feel about what Earl has done? _____

   _____

4. Is he able to convince Earl to talk about what he did? _____

   _____

5. Does Nathan seem interested in having a class free of confusion and disruption?

   _____

6. Do you think Nathan will have another talk with Earl about his behavior? _____

   Why or why not? _____

7. If he does, do you think it will cause Earl to think about his actions and perhaps
   regret them? _____

   _____

8. How does the friendship between Nathan and Earl make it easier for them to
   discuss Earl's behavior? _____

   _____

Talk About the Boys' Parents:

1. How does Earl feel about having his father find out what he has done? _____
   _____

2. Does Earl seem to respect his parents? _____

3. How can Earl's feeling about his parents be used to help him do the right thing
   in school?_____
   _____

4. How does Nathan seem to feel about his parents? _____
   _____

5. How do you think his relationship with his parents affects his in-school
   behavior?_____
   _____

Talk About Your Behavior:

1. Have you ever done anything like Earl did? _____ If so, did you think it was
   wrong at the time? _____ Do you think it is wrong now? _____

2. Would you yell into a classroom today?_____

Think and Write:

1. Write a note to Earl telling him what you think of his actions.

   Dear Earl,

   _____

   _____

   _____

   _____

   _____

   _____

   _____

   _____

   Yours truly,

   _____

2. Make a plan for Earl by completing the form that follows. Share it with your
   teacher.

Yo Dude! What's Up? (Scenario 33) and

What Did I Do? (Scenario 34)

A. Identify a behavior that Earl should change. _____
_____

B. Set a goal for Earl to work toward as he begins to make changes._____
_____
_____

C. Name a strategy that Earl can use to reach his goal. _____
_____
_____

D. Tell Earl how he can monitor his progress as he begins to make changes in his behavior. _____
_____
_____

Signature _____ Date _____

Rights versus Privileges

As you read, consider your answer to this question:

What is the difference between a right and a privilege?

▶ Marcus slams the door as he leaves the house and heads to the schoolyard to shoot some hoops. He dribbles his ball hard. Marcus is annoyed, and when he is annoyed he likes to shoot a few baskets to settle himself down. He thinks about stopping at Germaine's house to see if he wants to go along but decides against it. He really doesn't feel like talking to anybody else. What he feels like doing is punching somebody out.

Marcus is unhappy because his parents have told him that they will not buy him his favorite sneakers and that he is not allowed to buy them with his own money. His dad says the sneakers are overpriced and Marcus will outgrow them in a few months anyway. The subject is closed.

Who do they think they are, Marcus grumbles. His friends have the kind of sneakers they want. Their parents haven't stopped them from getting the one thing in the world they want more than anything else. Why should he wear plain sneakers when nobody else does?

Marcus talks to himself as he practices free throws. "I have my *rights.* I have the right to get the sneakers I want. I have some money saved. I can even help pay for them."

Is Marcus correct? Does he have a right to those sneakers? Before you answer, think for a few minutes about your life. Think about the people in your life such as your parents or guardians, your brothers and sisters, your friends. Think about the things you have, including your clothes, pets, bicycle, stereo, television set, computer, bedroom, even your sneakers—all the things that make your life as comfortable as it is.

Whether you have all of these things, some of them, or many more, you probably feel that you are *entitled* to each and every one of them. You feel that it is your right. But did you know that many of the things you enjoy are *privileges?*

Have you ever stopped to think about the difference between a right and a privilege? Of the experiences you have and the things you own, how many are yours because the *Constitution* says you are entitled to them? How many do you have simply because someone decides you should have them?

Getting back to the story, what do Marcus and his sneakers have to do with rights and privileges? And what do all these issues have to do with your own attitudes and behavior?

> **Constitution (of the United States):** document written in 1787 that lists basic laws and rights of the people
> **entitled:** have a claim
>
> **privileges:** special favors or advantages given to a person
> **rights:** something to which a person has a claim by law

Focus on the Problem

Talk About Marcus:

1. Why is Marcus unhappy? _____
_____

2. Do you think he should be able to get any pair of sneakers he wants? _____
Why?_____
_____

3. Why does Marcus want only a certain pair of sneakers?_____
_____

4. Would those expensive sneakers be considered a right or a privilege? _____
Explain. _____
_____

Talk About Yourself:

1. Have you ever been unable to get something you really wanted? _____
What was it? _____

2. How do you feel about your parents' putting limits on the amount of money you can spend on clothes or shoes?_____
_____

3. If you receive an item that is special or costs a lot of money, do you feel it is your right to have it, or do you see it as a special privilege? _____
_____

4. Name two things that you think are rights._____
_____

5. Name two things that you think are privileges. _____
_____

6. To what extent are your ideas about rights and privileges shaped by your classmates and friends?_____
_____

Talk About Your Classmates:

1. How do you feel about classmates and friends who seem to have more privileges than you do? _____

_____

2. How do your classmates react to others who seem to have extra privileges?

_____

_____

Talk and Write About Rights vs. Privileges:

1. Use the word "rights" in a sentence that shows you understand its meaning.

_____

_____

2. Use the word "privilege" in a sentence that shows you understand its meaning.

_____

_____

3. Discuss the following items with your teacher and classmates. Place a P in the space before items that are privileges and an R in the space before those that are rights.

___ a home to live in

___ a high school education

___ four new pairs of sneakers per year

___ free health insurance/medical care

___ a nice family car

___ a safe neighborhood

___ free transportation

___ free legal services

___ weekly movie money

___ an allowance of $15.00 or more per week

___ a college education

___ free hot lunches

___ presents on your birthday

___ name-brand clothes

___ a high school prom

___ police protection

___ a Big Brother or Big Sister

___ a chance to play basketball

4. Complete the following form. Share it with your teacher.

Goals, Strategies, and Monitoring Form 35

Rights Versus Privileges

A. The behavior I will change is ______________________________

____

B. My goal is to ______________________________

____

C. The strategy I will use for reaching my goal is ______________________________

____

____

D. While I work to reach my goal, I will monitor my progress by ______________________________

____

____

Signature ______________________________ Date ______________

Let's Get Mr. Smith in Trouble

As you read, consider your answer to this question:

Why would a student lie to harm a good teacher?

▶ "Amanda, I'm going to have to assign you a detention for your behavior," says Mr. Smith, looking sad. "We've talked about this before, and I've done everything I can to help you understand that certain behaviors are unacceptable in a classroom."

Amanda is having a conference with Mr. Smith at his desk as the other students copy their homework. She simply stares at him and does not respond. He makes some notes in his notebook and tells her when and where to report for her detention.

After school, Amanda calls her best friend. "Guess what, Jody. That old Mr. Smith gave me a detention for tomorrow. I have a note for my mom. He gets on my nerves. All I was doing was having a little fun. I don't see why I can't have a little fun. I do my work."

Jody asks, "Are you going to give the note to your mom?"

"I don't know. I'm already on punishment. It's supposed to end this weekend. If she finds out about this detention, you know what she'll do."

"Well," Jody says, "I have an idea. I don't know if you'll like it, though."

"I have to do something," Amanda answers. "What is it?"

"I know these girls who got their teacher in trouble when he was bugging them. They said it was easy. They figured that if he was busy trying to get himself out of trouble, he would leave them alone. And they figured he would probably let them do whatever they wanted afterward so they wouldn't report him again."

"How'd they do it?"

"Well, when they were about to get suspended for something they did, they made up a story about him. They said he touched them after school."

"But Mr. Smith didn't touch me. And I don't really want to get him in trouble. I just want him to leave me alone, " Amanda says.

"This is a good way to do it. Instead of giving the note to your mom, just tell her he touched you after school. Then all that other stuff will happen. He won't bother you any more," explains Jody.

"But it doesn't seem right," Amanda says. "I mean, Mr. Smith's okay. He's just too strict sometimes. I don't want to see him lose his job or anything."

Jody snaps, "What do you care what happens to him? Besides, he'll get out of it all right. He'll get a lawyer and everything. And at least it'll get him off your back."

Amanda says, before she hangs up the telephone, "I have to think about this one a little bit. I don't like the sound of it. I'll call you back later."

Focus on the Problem

Talk About Amanda:

1. What kind of person does Amanda seem to be? _____
   _____

2. Why is she upset with Mr. Smith? _____
   _____

Talk About Jody:

1. What kind of person does Jody seem to be? _____
   _____

2. What does she want Amanda to do?_____
   _____

3. How does Jody seem to feel about what she is telling Amanda to do? _____
   _____

Talk About Mr. Smith:

1. What kind of person does Mr. Smith seem to be? _____
   _____

2. Does he deserve the problem Jody wants to cause him? _____
   _____

Talk About Your Ideas:

1. Why is Amanda in trouble? _____
   _____

2. Do you think she will follow Jody's advice? _____ Why or why not? _____
   _____

3. Is Mr. Smith the cause of Amanda's problem? _____ Explain. _____
   _____

Take Part in a Role-Play:

(Amanda thinks about the idea Jody has for getting Mr. Smith in trouble. She calls Jody back.)

Amanda: Hi, Jody.

Jody: Oh, hi, Amanda. Are you going to talk to your mom about Mr. Smith?

Amanda: I haven't talked to her yet, but I'm going to. I've decided to tell her the truth.

Jody: The truth about what? About your detention?

Amanda: Yes.

Jody: Mandy, you must be losing it! You know she'll just put you back on punishment for who knows how long! I told you what you could do. I'll even help you. I'll say I walked in the door and saw him touch you. He won't have a chance!

Amanda: I know, and that's why I've decided against it. I mean, he bugs me and all. Sometimes he really gets on my nerves. But I don't want to get him in real trouble. He doesn't deserve to lose his job and everything.

Jody: But it's either him or you! Why should you be punished while he walks around free?

Amanda: Because he didn't do anything, remember? I was the one who was acting up. I'm just going to tell mom the whole truth and take whatever punishment she gives me. That stuff you're talking about is too serious for me. It's scary. I don't want to do it.

Jody: Well, Miss Mandy, don't ever say I didn't try to help you out. Enjoy your punishment!

Think and Write:

1. How can Jody make such a harmful suggestion without really giving it any thought?_____

2. Do you think Jody's serious idea is scaring Amanda into telling her mother about the detention? _____ Explain. _____
   _____

3. Do you think Amanda should tell her mother about Jody's suggestion? _____
   Why or why not?_____

4. What do you think will happen if Amanda's parents find out what Jody tried to get Amanda to do? _____

5. How do you feel about someone who lies to keep from having to face the consequences of his or her negative actions? _____

6. Complete the following form for Amanda and Jody. Share it with your teacher.

Let's Get Mr. Smith in Trouble

A. 1. Identify a behavior that Amanda should change. _____
_____

2. Set a goal for Amanda to aim for as she makes changes. _____
_____
_____

3. Name a strategy that Amanda can use to reach her goal. _____
_____
_____

4. Tell Amanda how she can monitor her progress as she makes changes in her
behavior. _____

B. 1. Identify a behavior that Jody should change. _____
_____

2. Set a goal for Jody to aim for as she makes changes. _____
_____

3. Name a strategy that Jody can use to reach her goal. _____
_____
_____

4. Tell Jody how she can monitor her progress as she makes changes in her
behavior. _____
_____

Signature _____ Date _____

Does It Really Matter What "They" Say?

As you read, consider your answer to this question:

Whose opinion of you is most important—yours or someone else's?

▶ **Read the story and complete the activities as though you yourself were confronting the situation.** Assume that you are an average student in a regular school. From time to time, you think about the actions that you and your friends take and the reasons why you take them. If the following things were happening to you, decide what your reactions would be.

A. You overhear two classmates talking about the way you dress. Does it matter what "they" say? How do you respond?

B. You know the answer to a question the teacher has asked, but no one else has raised a hand. What will "they" say if you let your intelligence show? What should you do?

C. You really don't want to act up in class anymore, but you've done it for so long. If you stop now, some of your classmates might call you strange or something worse. What can you do about what "they" say?

D. Your classmates are teasing the new kid in class and they want you to join in. You know it's wrong, but what will "they" say if you keep quiet or try to get them to stop?

E. You know you should head home because your parents have given you a set time to come in. But your friends are still out partying. If you go in before they do, what will "they" say?

F. Your friends want you to take something—just one small thing—the next time they shoplift. You know it's wrong, and you don't want to join in. But if you don't, what will "they" say?

Focus on the Problem

Talk and Write About Story A:

How do you feel when your friends say bad things about you?_____

_____

Talk and Write About Story B:

Do you ever avoid answering questions in class even when you know the correct answer? _____ If so, why do you do it? _____

_____

Talk and Write About Story C:

Identify two things that you know are wrong that you have done to please or impress your friends. _____

_____

Talk and Write About Story D:

1. If your friends want you to join in something you know is wrong, what do you tell them? _____

2. Do you think your friends or classmates respect you more if you always agree with them? _____ Why or why not? _____

_____

Talk and Write About Story E:

Are there times when you allow your friends to decide things for you that you should be deciding for yourself? _____ Explain. _____

_____

Talk and Write About Story F:

1. Do you ever allow your friends to talk you into doing something you know is wrong or harmful? _____ Why or why not? _____

2. Do you worry about things your friends might say or do if you don't let them control you? _____ Explain. _____

Think and Write:

1. Write a short role-play in which a friend tries to get you to do something you don't want to do. You are able to convince this friend that it is important for you to make up your own mind about the things you do.

2. Complete the form that follows. Share it with your teacher when you have finished.

Does It Really Matter What "They" Say?

A. 1. If my classmates or I have a problem with caring too much about what others think, our (my) goal is to _____

_____

2. These are two strategies that I (we) can use to reach my (our) goal.

a. _____

b. _____

3. These are two things that I (we) can do to monitor my (our) progress as I (we) make changes in my (our) behavior.

a. _____

b. _____

B. 1. If my classmates or I have a problem with trying to get others to do what we (I) want, our (my) goal is to _____

_____

_____

2. The strategy I (we) will use to reach my (our) goal is _____

_____

_____

3. I (We) will monitor my (our) progress as I (we) make changes in my (our) behavior by _____

_____

_____

Signature _____ Date _____

Revenge Is Mine!

As you read, consider your answer to this question:

What response is best when friends fail you in some way?

▶ Gerald's birthday is coming soon. He is planning a party and is excited about it. He has just started writing invitations to his best friends. . . .

Monday is a warm spring day. Gerald leaves home early so he can get to school and see his friends before classes start. He decides to stop in the restroom before going to his locker. As he is about to open the door, he overhears someone inside saying his name. He stops outside the door and listens. This is what he hears:

"I'm going to get Gerald! Who does he think he is? He calls himself my friend, but every time I turn around he's hanging out with Arnold. He knows I don't like Arnold because he runs with that dude over on the east end. Arnold and his friends tried to jump me when I went over there to visit my cousin. They said they're going to get me if I ever go back. If Gerald is my friend, he can't be Arnold's friend."

"Yeah, man, you ought to get Gerald. Show him who's in charge. Let him know he can't run around with just anybody. Let him know he has to stay around people

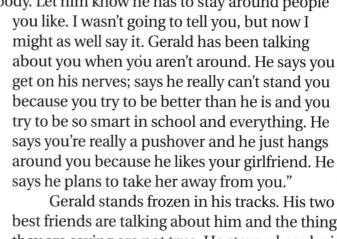

you like. I wasn't going to tell you, but now I might as well say it. Gerald has been talking about you when you aren't around. He says you get on his nerves; says he really can't stand you because you try to be better than he is and you try to be so smart in school and everything. He says you're really a pushover and he just hangs around you because he likes your girlfriend. He says he plans to take her away from you."

Gerald stands frozen in his tracks. His two best friends are talking about him and the things they are saying are not true. He stays where he is, feeling hurt and angry. He thinks, "These guys are my best buddies. Why are they saying these things? Should I go into the restroom and confront them? Should I turn around and go back home? Should I leave the building and hang out somewhere for the day while I think this over?"

Just then the door swings open. Gerald stands face to face with two people he thought were his friends. He looks at them quickly and asks himself, "What am I going to do? What *can* I do? What *should* I do?"

Focus on the Problem

Consider Gerald's Options:

1. What are some ways Gerald could handle the situation? _____
   _____

2. What do you think will happen if Gerald confronts his friends immediately? ____
   _____

Talk About the Friends:

1. Do you think Gerald's friends intended to hurt him when they said the things
   they did? _____ Explain. _____

2. Would Gerald's friends have let him know what was on their minds if he hadn't
   overheard it? _____
   _____

3. Do you feel Gerald should end the friendship? _____ Explain. _____
   _____

Discuss What Will Happen in the Future:

1. Do you think this problem will be settled soon or will Gerald have to deal with it
   for a while? _____ Explain. _____
   _____

2. Do you think Gerald has a plan for "paying his friends back"? _____
   _____

3. If so, what could that plan be? _____
   _____

Think and Write:

1. Write a short paragraph in which you explain what true friendship means.

2. Complete the monitoring form that follows Scenario 40.

Revenge Is Mine!

As you read, consider your answer to this question:

What response is best when friends fail you in some way?

▶ Ayana's birthday is coming soon. She is planning a party and is excited about it. She has just started writing invitations to her best friends. . . .

Monday is a warm spring day. Ayana leaves home early so she can get to school and see her friends before classes start. She decides to stop in the restroom before going to her locker. Just as she starts to open the door, she hears someone inside say her name. She stops outside the door. This is what she hears:

"I'm going to get Ayana. Who does she think she is? She acts like she's my friend, but I hear she's friendly with Brenda. She knows I don't like Brenda because she thinks she's better than anybody else. She and her friends act as if they don't want me around."

"Yeah, you ought to get her. I'll help you get her. She gets on my nerves anyway. We'll let her know she can't run around with just anybody. I wasn't going to tell you, but now I might as well say it. Ayana has been talking about you behind your back. She says she just hangs around with you so she can get her hands on your boyfriend. She says he is a real hunk and she wants him. She says she knows he likes her anyway. She talks about you whenever she gets a chance, and believe me, she isn't saying good things. Let's beat her up. I'll help you. We'll show her."

Ayana stands frozen in her tracks. Her two best friends are talking about her and the things they are saying are not true. She thinks, "Why are they saying these things? They are supposed to be my best friends." Ayana feels angry and hurt. She wonders, "Should I go into the restroom and confront them? Should I turn around and go back home? Should I leave the building and hang out somewhere for the day while I think this over?"

Just then the door swings open. Ayana stands face to face with two people she thought were her friends. She looks at them quickly and asks herself, "What am I going to do? What *can* I do? What *should* I do?"

Focus on the Problem

Consider Ayana's Options:

1. What are some ways Ayana could handle the situation? _____
   _____

2. What do you think will happen if Ayana confronts her friends immediately?
   _____

Talk About the Friends:

1. Do you think Ayana's friends intended to hurt her when they said the things they
   did? _____ Explain. _____

2. Would Ayana's friends have let her know what was on their minds if she hadn't
   overheard it? _____
   _____

3. Do you feel Ayana should end the friendship? _____ Explain. _____
   _____

Discuss What Will Happen in the Future:

1. Do you think this problem will be settled soon or will Ayana have to deal with it
   for a while? _____ Explain. _____
   _____

2. Do you think Ayana has a plan for "paying her friends back"? _____
   _____

3. If so, what could that plan be? _____
   _____

Think and Write:

1. Write a short paragraph in which you explain what true friendship means.

2. Complete the monitoring form that follows Scenario 40.

Ex-Friends Try to Ruin Your Party

As you read, consider your answer to this question:

What can you do when ex-friends try to "crash" your party?

▶ **Pretend that you are Gerald or Ayana (from the preceding scenario) as you read the story and complete the activities.** You overhear your best friends gossiping about you and making plans to "get" you. You decide not to confront them at school because it could cause a problem for you. Instead, you go ahead with plans for your birthday party and you don't invite them. You figure that should send the message that you don't like the things they're saying about you.

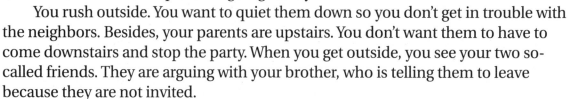

On the night of the party, everything is going great. You are excited and happy. Everyone says it's the best party they've been to in a long time. Suddenly, you hear voices outside. People are arguing loudly.

You rush outside. You want to quiet them down so you don't get in trouble with the neighbors. Besides, your parents are upstairs. You don't want them to have to come downstairs and stop the party. When you get outside, you see your two so-called friends. They are arguing with your brother, who is telling them to leave because they are not invited.

You are surprised. You figured your ex-friends knew about the party, but you didn't expect them to show up. "No, you can't come into my house unless I invite you in. You don't belong here," your brother is saying.

"Well," they say, "you'd better let us in because if you don't, we plan to turn this party out. If we can't party, then nobody can party." You and your brother look at each other. You think you smell alcohol on your ex-friends' breath. You don't have long to think. What can you do to keep things from getting out of hand?

Focus on the Problem

Talk and Write:

1. Do you think your ex-friends intend to do something serious? _____ Why?

   _____

2. How can you handle the situation quickly and quietly so that your party can continue?_____

Talk and Write About Your Options:

1. What options do you have? Consider those on this list and add others:

   a. chase away the intruders

   b. let the intruders in

   c. get your parents involved

   d. go inside and lock the door

   e. call the police

   f. fight

   g. (other idea)

   h. (other idea)

2. Decide which of the options on your list could lead to a positive solution to the problem and which could have negative consequences. Place a P in the space before each option you think is positive and an N in the space before each option you think is negative.

   a. ___ chase away the intruders   e. ___ call the police

   b. ___ let the intruders in   f. ___ fight

   c. ___ get your parents involved   g. ___ (other idea)

   d. ___ go inside and lock the door   h. ___ (other idea)

3. Discuss your list of options with your partner or group. As you do so, explain why you feel each option is a positive or a negative choice. On the basis of your discussion, write down what you think will happen if each option is carried through. As you talk and write, think about an answer to this question: What effect will my choice of options have on my relationships with my friends in school and in my neighborhood?

   a: _____

   b: _____

   c: _____

   d: _____

   e: _____

   f: _____

   g: _____

   h: _____

4. Complete the monitoring form that follows Scenario 40.

Confrontation!

As you read, consider your answer to this question:

How do you prepare yourself when you think you might be jumped?

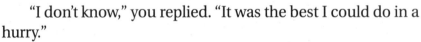

▶ **Pretend that you are Gerald or Ayana (from the preceding scenario) as you read the story and complete the activities.** It's now late spring. It has been a couple of weeks since your birthday party. You think back to that night—to the big mess that almost happened and to the way you and your brother were able to avoid it. You smile to yourself as you remember those events. . . .

When your ex-friends showed up at your party that night, smelling like alcohol and demanding that they be allowed into your house, you thought fast and made a decision that worked out well. You said to your brother, loudly so that everyone could hear, "I think I should go next door and get Captain Rogers."

In the light of the street lamp, you could see your brother give you a strange look. He said, "Oh, you mean the police officer who just moved in?"

"Yes," you said as you moved toward the house next door, "I think that's the best way to handle this situation."

Your brother nodded, "Yeah, that's probably the thing to do."

Your ex-friends started to leave, mumbling something like this: "We don't need you and your party. We can tell that nothing is going on in there, anyway. We're going to have a real party. Wait and see if you get invited to it."

As they walked away, your brother said, "Captain Rogers? Who's Captain Rogers?"

"I don't know," you replied. "It was the best I could do in a hurry."

Your brother laughed and replied, "Well, it worked."

You come back to the present. It's nice outside, and school will soon be over for the year. You haven't had a chance to do any hanging out because you've been busy with final exams and getting school projects finished and helping out around the house. The letter about your summer job arrived a few days ago, and today you have a job interview.

You turn a corner and come face to face with your two ex-friends and a couple of their friends. They seem to be just hanging around. You get just a little nervous but you decide to pretend there's no problem.

"Hi. What's up? Do you have job interviews, too? That's where I'm headed now." When they don't answer, you decide that you have done your best, so you step around them and go on your way.

Then you hear, "Yo! Wait up!" You turn around, not knowing what to expect. . . .

Focus on the Problem

Talk About What Is Happening:

1. How should you handle an unexpected confrontation like this that could be dangerous for you? _____

2. Could your ex-friends know about your appointment and be waiting for you?

   _____

Talk About Your Feelings:

1. Are you afraid? _____ Why or why not? _____

   _____

2. Are you feeling a little bit annoyed because your ex-friends keep turning up in your life? _____ Explain. _____

Talk About Your Options:

1. You have just walked past your ex-friends, when they call out to you. You have to make a decision—what will you do? Consider these options add others to the list.

   a. Continue walking as if you did not hear them call to you.

   b. Walk back to where they are standing and see what happens.

   c. Stop walking and wait for them to catch up with you.

   d. (other idea)

2. Discuss each option with your partner or group and write down what you think would happen if each option were carried through.

   a: _____

   b: _____

   c: _____

   d: _____

Think and Write:

1. Write an ending for this scenario, drawing on the options you just considered. Write it as a role-play if you choose. Begin as the friends stand together on the street.

2. Complete the following monitoring form. Share it with your teacher when you have finished.

Revenge Is Mine! (Scenario 38A and 38B)
Ex-Friends Try to Ruin Your Party (Scenario 39)
and
Confrontation! (Scenario 40)

A. The behavior I will change is _____

_____

B. My goal is to _____

_____

C. The strategy I will use for reaching my goal is _____

_____

_____

D. While I work to reach my goal, I will monitor my progress by _____

_____

_____

Signature _____ Date _____

Appendix

Answer Key for Introductory Lesson

"Complete a Word Search"

```
S E L F R E S P E C T C H A L L E N G E A
A E B C D E F R E L A T I O N S H I P S C
C G L H R E S O L V E I J K F L M N O T C
O P Q F R S T U V W X O P T I O N Y Z E E
N A B C D I S R U P T I O N D E C F P E P
S A I J K I C O N F R O N T L M N U Q M T
E C O R P E S A C O O P E R A T E C S P A
Q R H S E L F C O N F I D E N C E S I R B
U D U O V W X Y I Z A B C M D E F N T E L
E I H I J K L M P N O P Q O R S E I S E E
N S A U V C C O N F L I C T W N M G V P O
C R T Z G A E B C D E I F G H I O A E O I
E U T R O R E S P E C T N K B L N T N S R
S P I O A P S E L F E S T E E M I I O S A
R T T S L T T U V W X Y Z A H B T V D I N
A B U C S R E A C T I O N D A E O E D B E
E F D G H I J G K L M N O P V Q R S T L C
U V E W X Y Z A Y B C D E F I G H I J E S
D I S C I P L I N E K P O S O T I V E L S
C O N F R O N T A T I O N M R E G N A N E
```

Lesson Plan Form
Completed for Scenario 2

Class:_____ Date :_____

Teacher: _____

Topic of Lesson: Creating a Better Classroom Atmosphere (Scenario 2)

Objective(s):   To teach students to examine problems that occur in the classroom

Materials: *Help Me Decide!;* copy of Scenario 2 for each student; list of behavior-related words; list of goals, strategies, monitoring devices

Procedure:
Vocabulary:

1. Review meanings and use of relevant words from special word list as needed.

Opening Question:

2. Allow students to suggest ways in which they can help solve problems in the classroom. List ideas on chalkboard.

Scenario:

3. Read the scenario aloud to the class.

Guided Large-Group Discussion:

4. Invite students to compare briefly the ideas listed on the chalkboard with the ideas presented in the scenario.

5. Have students discuss the disruptive behaviors displayed in Mrs. Wiggins's class.

6. Have students discuss the disruptive behaviors displayed in their own class.

Small-Group Discussion:

7. Have students meet in small groups. Direct group members to discuss their ideas and complete the written activities. Actively supervise this effort.

Guided Large-Group Discussion:

8. Have students break out of their groups for a whole-class discussion. Guide the discussion by asking questions from among those included with the scenario.

Follow-Up Activity:

9. Invite students to participate in a role-play.

Assessment Form:

10. Guide students in selecting appropriate goals, strategies, and monitoring ideas for completion of "Goals, Strategies, and Monitoring" form. Have students begin work on form.

Role-Plays

Creating a Role-Play

Role-plays should be very short—a few minutes at most. In addition to teacher-written role-plays, consider student-written ones. Students working individually, in pairs, or in small groups can create a variety of role-plays by looking at the same scenario events in different ways. Here are some basic steps to follow:

1. Choose the incident, the behavior, or the activity that will be the focus of the role-play.

2. Decide whether the incident will re-enact story events or predict future events.

3. Decide on the point to be made (e.g., showing specific examples of negative behavior and then modeling appropriate behavior; suggesting possible resolutions to problems; predicting future actions of students or characters).

4. Limit the number of characters; stick mainly to the characters who are in the story.

5. Turn any available conversation from the story into dialogue.

6. Add additional dialogue if necessary, following the story line.

7. Write the role-play on the chalkboard or copy it onto paper and hand it out to participants.

Presenting a Role-Play

1. Explain to students what they will be doing and why (e.g., showing a negative incident and then showing a positive version of the same incident).

2. Allow as many groups to participate as time will allow.

3. Invite students to discuss each role-play in two ways after it has been presented: the substance of what has been said, and the manner in which the role-play was presented.

4. If it can be done without creating problems, allow small groups or individuals to critique each other, offering positive suggestions for change.

Other Considerations

1. Depending upon the nature of the role-play, it may be effective to quietly arrange with a group or with individual students to present a role-play on cue, without the other students having been told what is about to happen.

2. When students become more proficient, impromptu role-plays may evolve from the discussions, particularly if the teacher participates.

Sample Role-Plays

Following are several short role-plays based on Scenario 2.

(1) Role-Play: Isolating Negative Classroom Behavior
Scenario 2: Creating a Better Classroom Atmosphere

Characters: Mrs. (or Mr.) Wiggins, Jonathan, Theo, Katrice, the class

(The class is at work. Mrs. Wiggins is talking with Sonya.)

Jonathan: *(Talking to himself half out loud.)* Man! I don't know why I can't get this right. It's boring, anyway. *(He snatches a sheet of paper from his notebook and goes toward the trash can. As he does so, he trips over Theo's feet and falls.)*

The class: *(Students stop working and watch what happens.)*

Jonathan: Watch it, man!

Theo: Sorry, man. I didn't mean to do that.

Katrice: Yes, you did. You know you did.

Theo: Mind your own business, bird-brain.

Katrice: Who are you calling bird-brain, pea-head?

Wiggins: Theo, Katrice, Jonathan, first warning. Let's get back to work, class. Jonathan, let's see if we can't figure out where you're having difficulty.

(Katrice and Theo stare at each other but they don't say anything else. The class goes back to work.)

(2) Role-Play: Modeling Appropriate Classroom Behavior
Scenario 2: Creating a Better Classroom Atmosphere

Characters: Mrs. (or Mr.) Wiggins, Jonathan, the class

(The class is at work. All of the students have a partner except Jonathan. Mrs. Wiggins is talking with Sonya.)

Jonathan: *(Talking to himself half out loud)* Man! I don't know why I can't get this right. *(He raises his hand. While he waits for the teacher, Jonathan turns a page in his notebook and heads a clean sheet of paper.)*

Wiggins: *(Walks over to him to see how she can help.)*

Jonathan: Mrs. Wiggins, I can't figure this problem out. I did it the way we did the sample on the board but it's not coming out right.

Wiggins: Okay, Jonathan. I know your partner is absent today, so why don't I work as your partner? Let's see what you're doing. *(She begins working with Jonathan.)*

The class: *(Students continue working with their partners.)*

(3) Role-Play: Isolating Negative Classroom Behavior
Scenario 2: Creating a Better Classroom Atmosphere

Characters: Mrs. (or Mr.) Wiggins, Tremaine, Katrice, Jonathan, Theo, the class

(Mrs. Wiggins is talking to the class. Everyone is quiet. The door swings open. Tremaine strolls in. He does not have a notebook, a pencil, or paper.)

Wiggins: Good morning, Tremaine.

Tremaine: *(Looks at the teacher but does not say anything.)*

Wiggins: *(Speaks quietly.)* Tremaine, where are your materials? And you know you have to bring in a note when you come to class late.

Tremaine: Get out of my face! I don't have a note. And I don't have anything else! Leave me alone!

Wiggins: Tremaine, you know the rules. We all agreed on them. If you don't follow them, you know there will be consequences.

Tremaine: *(He turns and starts out of the classroom, mumbling to himself.)* Who does she think she is? So I don't have any supplies, or a note. So what? I'm not staying for anybody's detention! *(He slams the door.)*

The class: *(Students laugh loudly.)*

Wiggins: Okay, class, I'm glad you didn't say anything to Tremaine. But what did you just do?

Katrice: We laughed out loud.

Wiggins: That's right. What's wrong with that?

Theo: We were supposed to mind our own business.

Jonathan: And let you handle problems.

Wiggins: Great! I'm glad you remember the rules. Let's all work a little harder at following them. We'll talk some more about this during our next behavior lesson. Now, let's get back to work. I'll speak with Tremaine later.

(4) Role Play: Modeling Appropriate Classroom Behavior
Scenario 2: Creating a Better Classroom Atmosphere

Characters: Mrs. (or Mr.) Wiggins, Tremaine, the class

(Mrs. Wiggins is talking to the class. Everyone is quiet. The door swings open. Tremaine strolls in. He does not have a notebook, a pencil, or paper.)

Wiggins: Good morning, Tremaine.

Tremaine: Good morning. *(He heads toward the teacher.)*

Wiggins: *(Speaks quietly.)* Tremaine, where are your materials? And you know you have to bring in a note when you come to class late.

Tremaine: I know. I had a problem at home today. I just got to school. Would it be okay if I explained it to you after class?

Wiggins: Yes, Tremaine. Stay for a few minutes at the end of class and we'll talk.

Tremaine: All right. *(He goes to his seat.)*

(The class continues to work.)

Role-Play Scoring Rubric

Student _____ Date _____

Character Played _____ Scenario_____

	RATING INDICATOR			
CRITERIA:	**0**	**1**	**2**	
	Never	**Sometimes**	**Always**	**SCORE**
Made the character believable	_____	_____	_____	_____
Helped everyone understand the problem	_____	_____	_____	_____
Spoke lines clearly	_____	_____	_____	_____
Used appropriate gestures props, etc.	_____	_____	_____	_____
Total score	_____	_____	_____	_____

Ideas for Setting Goals, Choosing Strategies, and Learning to Self-Monitor

Goals

Practice Desired General School Behaviors:

Accept responsibility for the actions you take.

Act to keep school property clean.

Attend school regularly.

Bring needed materials to class.

Do a good deed whenever possible.

Do your homework.

Encourage positive interactions.

Get to school on time.

Give yourself credit for skills and knowledge acquired.

Hand assignments in on time.

Organize your locker/bookbag.

Participate in school clubs/ organizations.

Refuse to carry a weapon.

Refuse to copy homework.

Refuse to share your homework.

Show respect for yourself and others.

Practice Desired Classroom Behaviors:

Accept responsibility for the actions you take.

Actively seek to meet the goals you set.

Avoid instigating trouble.

Avoid making fun of others.

Concentrate on your schoolwork.

Contribute to class lessons.

Do no boasting.

Do no fighting.

Do no stealing

Get to class on time.

Hand assignments in on time.

Keep hands and feet off others.

Keep promises.

Listen actively when others are talking.

Make no threats.

Make positive statements.

Organize notebook and other materials.

Raise your hand before speaking (when required.)

Respect the property of others.

Respond when called upon.

Seek help as needed.

Show respect to your teacher and classmates.

Speak in an acceptable manner.

Spend required amount of time on each task.

Spread no rumors.

Start classwork as soon as it is assigned.

Take an active role in small groups.

Take an active role in your education.

Take part in discussions.

Tell the truth.

Treat others as you would like to be treated.

Tutor other students (with permission).

Strategies

Accept praise from teachers and other adults.

Accept or ask for a leadership role.

Apologize willingly when necessary.

Ask for a change of seating if needed.

Ask to have longer tasks split into shorter tasks.

Ask to be placed on a daily report.

Ask the teacher for help in learning to focus.

Copy class rules into a notebook and review them from time to time.

Count positive interactions with classmates and adults.

Develop a personal calendar.

Get notes or permission slips signed the night before.

Help friends/classmates to do positive things.

Leave home fifteen minutes earlier than usual.

Let everyone know you are making positive changes.

Make a contract with your teacher.

Make and follow a detailed schedule for doing homework.

Observe teacher's silent cues to change behavior.

Organize your time by making a schedule.

Plan an earlier bedtime.

Practice focusing on your assignments.

Practice listening to directions the first time they are given.

Practice making quick starts on class assignments.

Prepare school clothes the night before.

Request written step-by-step directions from the teachers as needed.

Role-play acceptable behaviors.

Work cooperatively with your partner or group members.

Work hard even when there are no incentives or rewards.

Self-Monitoring

Arrange with your teacher to share results periodically.

Keep a daily goal sheet.

Maintain a daily journal detailing your efforts to make positive changes.

Maintain a daily or weekly chart showing positive changes.

Maintain a daily or weekly graph showing positive changes.

Report documented results to your teacher or other adult.

Request feedback from your teacher or other adult.

Share your efforts with a parent or other adult whom you respect.

Track your success in reaching the goals you've set.

Alternative Forms for Lessons

The forms that follow may be used instead of, or in addition to, those that appear on the last page of many of the lessons. Several types of forms are included: a *Contract* form; a *Pledge* form; a *Goal Statement* form; a daily goal sheet for general use; a sample completed daily goal sheet; line graph form for counting occasions of negative behavior; line graph form for counting decreasing occasions of negative behavior; line graph form for counting increasing occasions of positive behavior; and a bar graph form for monitoring homework completion.

Contract

The sample *Goals, Strategies, and Monitoring form* may be completed as part of one of the lessons in this manual or it may be used independently to address other classroom behaviors. The form is designed to be filled in by the student with very little input from the teacher. Middle-grade students can use the form as a guide in constructing contracts for themselves. They can also use it to keep track of behaviors targeted in their contracts, which means the teacher need only give them cursory attention.

My Pledge

Initially, work with the whole group. Read and discuss the pledge. Then divide the class into small groups for pledge-writing activities. Have students begin the *Pledge* form. Plan time for discussions centered around the achievement of goals established in the original pledge or an alternate written by the class. The class or group might wish to adopt as its own the pledge presented. If everyone agrees, you might plan to recite it each day. Alternatively, writing one's own pledge can be a valuable cooperative or competitive activity for groups. Students are generally more willing to learn a pledge and recite it regularly if they participate in writing it. While all students may not take the idea of a pledge seriously, the pledge can at least serve as a point of reference during discussions of appropriate and inappropriate behavior.

Daily Goal Sheet

For students who need the additional support of recording their accomplishments every day, consider having them complete a daily goal sheet. The idea here is that students set specific behavioral or academic goals for the day and receive points for reaching them. The long-range goal should remain the same for as long as it takes the student to make progress. The daily goal can remain the same or change daily, depending upon whether the student actually attains it. This activity requires only a few minutes, yet can be highly effective. Checking to determine goal attainment can occur at the end of the day or at the beginning of the next, just before students fill out the new sheet. (See the suggested goals, strategies, and monitoring ideas presented earlier in this Appendix.)

Line Graph Forms

Completing line graphs for countable behaviors lets students assess their behaviors on a weekly, bi-weekly, or longer basis. This format provides students with an easy way to count decreasing negative behaviors or increasing positive behaviors and to note trends as they occur. These graphs can be maintained for any countable behavior and can be kept in student notebooks and routinely shared with you, the teacher.

Bar Graph Form (for Homework Completion)

The bar graph form for monitoring homework completion is easy for students to use. Completing the form lets them keep track of their homework assignments for a two-week period. Maintaining the graphs over time provides a useful snapshot of students' homework habits.

Contract Form

Scenario 1

_____

A. The behavior I would like to change is_____

_____

_____

B. My goal for change is to _____

_____

by (target date) _____

C. These are my strategies for reaching my goals (check off when completed):

    1. _____

    2. _____

    3. _____

    4. _____

D. This is the way I will monitor my progress (check off when completed):

I will _____

I will _____

I will _____

E. Comments: _____

_____

_____

Signature _____ Date _____

My Pledge

I hold in my hands the power to change my behavior;

I hold in my hands the power to change my life.

I know that I have options.

I will use what I am learning to choose the options

That will help me become a better student

And a better person. These are the things I will do:

I will come to school with a positive attitude.

I will do my classwork and my homework.

I will carry myself with dignity and pride.

I will respect the rights of others.

I will use my power to make a better life

For myself and those around me.

Nothing will stop me!

This is my pledge.

Focus on the Pledge

Talk About the Pledge:

1. What is a pledge? _____

   _____

2. To whom are you making this pledge? _____

3. If your behavior changes, what else might change? _____

   _____

4. What is the "power" that is referred to in the pledge? _____

   _____

5. What can happen if you carefully choose your options? _____

   _____

6. If you choose to live by this pledge, you promise to do five things. List them below:

   a. _____

   b. _____

   c. _____

   d. _____

   e. _____

Think and Write:

1. With your classmates, write another pledge. Use the pledge you have just discussed as a guide when writing. Perhaps you can think of new ways to express the ideas found in the first pledge. Or, perhaps you can come up with other ideas that you would like to include in your pledge.

2. Make a behavior goal sheet for your new pledge. Share it with your teacher.

3. Copy your pledge onto a large sheet of poster board or paper and place it on the wall in your classroom where you and your classmates can see it whenever you need to do so.

4. With your partner, group, or classmates, choose either the pledge you read earlier or the pledge you wrote and memorize it. Plan to say it every day. Think about its meaning during your classes.

5. Keep a copy of your pledge in your notebook and reread it from time to time.

Daily Goal Sheet

Strategies for Improving Behavior

My long-range goal is to _____

_____

The strategy I will use to reach my long-range goal is to _____

_____

_____

My goal for today is to _____

_____

The strategy I will use to reach my goal for today is:

_____

_____

_____

I will monitor my progress by _____

_____

_____

_____

Signature _____

Date _____

Number of points earned today: _____

Daily Goal Sheet

(Completed Sample)

Strategies for Improving Behavior

My long-range goal is to get into an academic high school.

_____

The strategy I will use to reach my long-range goal is to work on my behavior so that it is as good as my academic work.

My goal for today is to set some rules for myself to help me get off to a good start

The strategy I will use to reach my goal for today is: tell my friends my plan and ask them to stand by me and help me make my plan work.

I will monitor my progress by recording at the end of the day the number of points I have earned. I will share my form with my teacher.

Signature _____

Date _____

Number of points earned today: _____

Strategies for Improving Behavior

A. Choose a negative behavior that you want to change.

The negative behavior I want to change is _____

_____

B. Count the number of times (from zero to ten) that your selected negative behavior occurs each day for one week. Use that information to complete this graph.

Occasions of Negative Behavior During a One-Week Period

GRAPH I

	M	T	W	Th	F
10					
9					
8					
7					
6					
5					
4					
3					
2					
1					
0					

C. After completing your graph, fill in the information that follows. _____

1. I have recorded the number of times that the selected negative behavior occurred and completed the graph. I have learned that I showed the behavior _____ times during the week.

2. My goal is to cut this behavior to _____ times per week.

3. I will work for _____ weeks to change this behavior. I will use the strategies I have learned and keep a record of what happens.

4. When this page is complete, I will share it with my teacher.

Signature _____ Date _____

Line Graph Form for Counting Decreasing Occasions
of Negative Behavior (1 week)

A. Use learned strategies to cut the number of times you show a selected negative behavior.

B. As your negative behavior decreases, record these changes on Graph 2A.

Decreasing Occasions of Negative Behavior During
a One-Week Period

GRAPH 2A

	M	T	W	Th	F
10					
9					
8					
7					
6					
5					
4					
3					
2					
1					
0					

C. After completing Graph 2A, fill in the blanks that follow.

1. On Monday, I showed the selected negative behavior ____ times.

2. On Tuesday, I showed the selected negative behavior ____ times.

3. On Wednesday, I showed the selected negative behavior ____ times.

4. On Thursday, I showed the selected negative behavior ____ times.

5. On Friday, I showed the selected negative behavior ____ times.

D. Choose the statement that applies to you.

_____ From Monday to Friday, the number of times I showed the selected negative behavior decreased.

_____ From Monday to Friday, the number of times I showed the selected negative behavior remained the same.

_____ From Monday to Friday, the number of times I showed the selected negative behavior increased.

Line Graph Form for Counting Increasing Occasions
of Positive Behavior (1 week)

A. Select a positive behavior to replace the negative behavior you want to change.

_____

B. Use learned strategies to increase the number of times you show the selected positive behavior.

C. On Graph 2B, record the positive changes you are making.

Increasing Occasions of Positive Behavior During a One-Week Period

GRAPH 2B

	M	T	W	Th	F
10					
9					
8					
7					
6					
5					
4					
3					
2					
1					
0					

D. Choose the statement that applies to you.

_____ From Monday to Friday, the number of times I showed the selected positive behavior decreased.

_____ From Monday to Friday, the number of times I showed the selected positive behavior remained the same.

_____ From Monday to Friday, the number of times I showed the selected positive behavior increased.

Strategies for Improving Behavior

Bar Graph Form for Monitoring Daily Homework Completion (2 weeks)

Use this graph to measure assignments given and completed for a two-week period. Build a bar graph by filling a "#Given" space each time you get an assignment and a "#Done" space each time you complete an assignment.

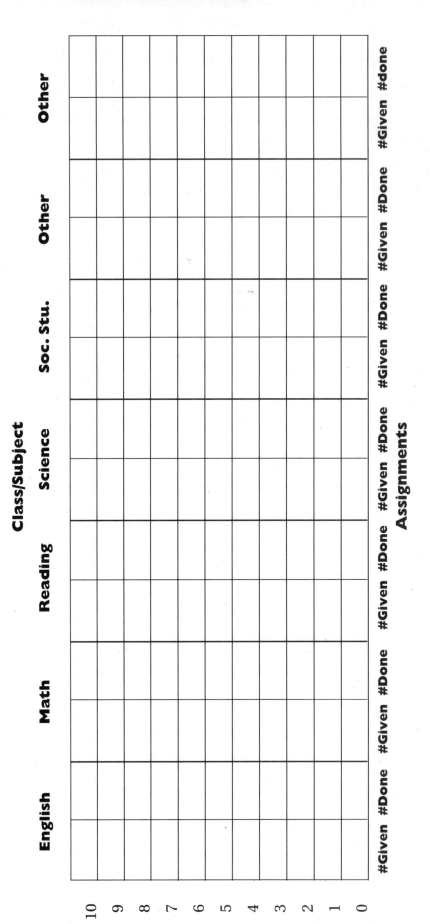

Class/Subject

	English		Math		Reading		Science		Soc. Stu.		Other		Other	
10															
9															
8															
7															
6															
5															
4															
3															
2															
1															
0															

#Given #Done #Given #Done #Given #Done #Given #Done #Given #Done #Given #Done #Given #done

Assignments

Signature _____ Date _____